LOOK UP

HILARY BERNSTEIN

LOOK UP

200 PRAYERS
TO ENCOURAGE A
YOUNG WOMAN'S HEART

BARBOUR
PUBLISHING

Print ISBN 978-1-64352-914-1

Published by Barbour Publishing, Inc., 1810 Barbour Drive, Uhrichsville, Ohio 44683, www.barbourbooks.com

Our mission is to inspire the world with the life-changing message of the Bible.

Member of the
Evangelical Christian
Publishers Association

Printed in China.

INTRODUCTION

It's easy to focus on what's happening around you. Concerns about school, friends, or current events steal your attention. Wishes and dreams dominate your thoughts. You find yourself spending a lot of time thinking about what happened in the past and what could happen in the future. While it's normal to focus on your hopes, hurts, and happiness, sometimes those thoughts can end up crowding out the Giver of all your good gifts. Your heavenly Father loves you so much, and He wants you to know and experience His love, peace, and hope. As you start looking up and focusing on the Lord, you'll be filled with His encouragement and peace. You'll understand your own incredible worth as you realize how very special you are and how much you are loved by the Lord. When you read His Word, think about what He is trying to tell you, and figure out what it personally means to you; you'll be changed in an amazing way. My hope for you is that the scripture and prayers in this book will turn your heart and mind to God's truth—and that you'll look up and fix your attention and affection on our Lord.

In Christ's great love,
Hilary Bernstein

WATCH FOR THE LORD

But as for me, I will watch for the Lord.
I will wait for the God Who saves me.
My God will hear me.
MICAH 7:7 NLV

Lord God, I'm so thankful You hear me! And I love that You are the God who saves me. Because of that, I will watch and wait for You in my life. When I'm tempted to be impatient or to rush things, please strengthen my heart to keep watching for the ways You're at work. Please help me keep waiting on You and for You. I certainly can't save myself. I don't want to trust in myself, and I don't want to forget that You have a plan and purpose for everything. Please help me remember to look up in the middle of any situation and remember You. Please keep my heart focused on You. I love You, Lord! In Jesus' name I pray, amen.

I WILL WATCH AND WAIT FOR THE LORD.

THE LIFTER OF MY HEAD

But you, O LORD, are a shield about me,
my glory, and the lifter of my head.
PSALM 3:3 ESV

Lord, sometimes when I get discouraged or scared, it's so easy to focus on my feelings and circumstances. When I think about what's negative, it's almost like getting stuck in a pit. Please help me remember that You're my shield—You're my protection and defense! And You lift my head. When I'm overwhelmed, You're the One who helps me see beyond myself. When I want to look down and focus on all that's happening all around me, You're the One who holds my head high. You're my glory. I'll never find glory in myself. And I'll never be able to get my act together to hold my own head up when life gets really tough. But You will. In the middle of challenges, I pray I'll trust You as my shield, glory, and lifter of my head. In Jesus' name I pray, amen.

THE LORD WILL PROTECT, COMFORT,
AND ENCOURAGE ME.

THAT WAS QUICK!

Before they call I will answer;
while they are still speaking I will hear.
ISAIAH 65:24 NIV

Almighty God, I'm amazed at how You completely know me—and still choose to love me! Before a word is even on my lips, You know what I'll say. Sometimes when I pray, I notice You answer me right away. I love it when You do that! It's a huge comfort to know that You hear me. And it's a comfort that what I say really matters to You. Sometimes it feels like I don't have a voice in the world. People around me just don't seem to listen to me or hear what I have to say. But You hear every word I pray, and You're ready to answer me. I pray You'll help me notice when You do answer. Thank You for hearing me—and listening to me. You are the God who hears! In Jesus' name I pray, amen.

GOD HEARS MY PRAYERS.

PEACEFUL SLEEP

I will lie down and sleep in peace.
O Lord, You alone keep me safe.
PSALM 4:8 NLV

O Lord, sometimes it's really hard to fall asleep! My mind is weighed down by a million thoughts. I can't stop thinking about what happened today or what might happen tomorrow. I analyze different relationships and wonder what I can do differently. I replay things I've said or done, and wish I could change what's in the past. I even think about danger—what might happen to me? The fantastic thing I desperately need to remember is that You are the One who keeps me safe. I don't have to toss and turn in fear. I don't even have to worry about nightmares. I can actually sleep in peace! A peaceful night of sleep sounds so wonderful. I pray I'll rest in Your protection and peacefully fall—and stay—asleep. Thank You for filling me with peace I could never achieve on my own. In Jesus' name I pray, amen.

I CAN SLEEP IN PEACE BECAUSE
THE LORD KEEPS ME SAFE.

WHY WORRY?

*Can any one of you by worrying
add a single hour to your life?*
MATTHEW 6:27 NIV

Father, I admit it's easy to worry. There's so much that's out of my control! What is happening in the world? What is happening in my life? What's happening to my family? What's happening to my friends? What if my life is completely changed just because of what I do at school? What will happen if I don't make the cut—either with friends, clubs, teams, or grades? I could spend a lot of time worrying about what might or might not happen. But that would be a waste. Please help me remember my worrying won't accomplish anything and it won't change reality. Whenever I worry, I'm not fully trusting You. I do believe You can bring good from situations that seem pretty bad, so I pray I'll trust You. Please give me peace and strength to face whatever comes my way. And please help me remember that worrying usually means I'm imagining the worst possibilities. I'd rather trust You for the best. Amen.

WORRYING DOESN'T ACCOMPLISH ANYTHING
EXCEPT TAKING MY FOCUS OFF THE LORD.

MINDFUL OF ME

*When I consider your heavens, the work
of your fingers, the moon and the stars,
which you have set in place, what is mankind
that you are mindful of them, human
beings that you care for them?*

PSALM 8:3–4 NIV

Creator God, I'm amazed when I think about all
You've made. You created this entire universe out
of nothing! You've intricately made and know
every living thing in this world, including me.
What might be even more amazing is the way
You're mindful of every human. You pay attention to us. It's not like You've slipped into auto-
pilot or You've zoned out. No, You know what's
going on each and every moment. And You care
for us and about us. Nothing I do escapes Your
attention. Just as You're always paying attention
to me, I want to pay attention to You. I want to
care about You too. I may not be able to do a
perfect job like You. In fact, I might falter a lot.
But I pray I'll still try. I love You, Lord! In Jesus'
name I pray, amen.

GOD ALWAYS PAYS ATTENTION
TO ME AND CARES FOR ME.

COMFORT, HOPE, AND STRENGTH

Now may our Lord Jesus Christ Himself and God our Father, who has loved us and given us eternal comfort and good hope by grace, comfort and strengthen your hearts in every good work and word.

2 THESSALONIANS 2:16–17 NASB

God my Father, thank You for loving me! When I feel discouraged and weak, please strengthen my heart and give me comfort in the ways that only You can. You can fill me with hope. Thank You! Through my Lord Jesus Christ, You can give me comfort that lasts forever. Thank You! I pray I'll be able to clearly see the way You're working in my life. And I pray that You'll use both the things I do and the things I say in the lives of others. As You've filled my life with Your love, please help me pour it out on people around me. Please help me share Your comfort with my family and friends—even with strangers. In Jesus' name I pray, amen.

GOD LOVES ME! AND HE GIVES ME
HOPE, COMFORT, AND STRENGTH.

THANK YOU!

*I will give thanks to the Lord with all
my heart. I will tell of all the great things
You have done. I will be glad and full
of joy because of You. I will sing praise
to Your name, O Most High.*

PSALM 9:1–2 NLV

Lord, no matter what's happening in my life right now, thank You. I'm glad that whatever seems to stand in my way, I can still be full of joy. How is that even possible? It's all because of You! When it seems difficult to be glad, I choose to praise You anyway. And I'll give You thanks with all of my heart! Not just a little part. And I'll thank and praise You not because I feel like I should, but because I want to. I'm truly thankful for all of the great things You've done in my life. And I'm thankful for the things You've done for me. You've blessed me with so much I don't deserve. Every good and perfect gift has come from You. I know that, and I truly appreciate it. Thank You!

GOD HAS DONE GREAT THINGS FOR ME,
SO I CHOOSE TO THANK AND PRAISE HIM.

THE GOD WHO SEES

She gave this name to the Lord who spoke to her: "You are the God who sees me," for she said, "I have now seen the One who sees me."
GENESIS 16:13 NIV

Lord God, You see me. You know me. And You choose to love me anyway. I can't get away from Your presence. Sometimes, I might think that I want to be by myself, but really, I would be truly lonely. Thank You that You never leave me alone. Thank You for always seeing. You are the God who sees me. You see what I'm facing and You're there for me. I don't have to worry about going through this life all by myself. You'll never leave me or forsake me. Even if other people turn their back on me, You never will. I don't have to pretend I'm someone else with You—You know me completely, flaws and strengths and all. I'm grateful that You are the God who sees me. In Jesus' name I pray, amen.

GOD IS THE ONE WHO SEES ME.

THE GOD WHO HEARS

Hear my words, O Lord. Think about my crying. Listen to my cry for help, my King and my God. For I pray to you.
PSALM 5:1–2 NLV

Father God, just as You see me, I'm glad You also hear me. You hear my prayers, and You hear and know my emotions. You know when I'm happy and when I'm sad. Lord, when I'm scared or feeling like I'm in trouble or danger, please listen to my cry for help! Please give me discernment to make wise decisions. Please show me what I should do. I know You're there, always. And instead of just being there as the all-knowing, ever-present God, please help me sense that You're there and that You care. As You listen to my crying, I pray You'll comfort me in some way. I love You, trust You, and would love You to reassure me that You really do care. In Jesus' name I pray, amen.

WHEN I PRAY HONESTLY TO GOD,
HE WILL HEAR MY WORDS.

THREE THINGS

*Rejoice always, pray without ceasing,
in everything give thanks; for this is the
will of God for you in Christ Jesus.*
1 THESSALONIANS 5:16–18 NASB

Father, sometimes I'm not sure what Your will is. But Your Word clearly tells me about Your will for me. It's to rejoice—and not just some of the time, but always. Just like I should rejoice all the time, I also should pray all the time. Why? Because You hear and answer my prayers! If I spend my waking hours praying to You, I'm reminded that You're God and I'm not. I can look for Your guidance instead of trying to live life on my own. The other thing I need to do in every situation is to give You thanks. Thank You when times are easy and everything seems to be going my way. And thank You when times are hard. My challenges and difficulties are the best opportunities to trust You and see You at work. Thank You that Your will for me in Christ Jesus is to rejoice, pray, and give thanks. In Jesus' name I pray, amen.

GOD'S WILL FOR ME IS TO
REJOICE, PRAY, AND THANK HIM.

GLADNESS AND JOY

But let all who take refuge in you be glad;
let them ever sing for joy. Spread your
protection over them, that those who
love your name may rejoice in you.

PSALM 5:11 NIV

Lord, I am so glad I can take refuge in You. You're my safe place! You'll protect me! I pray that You will spread Your protection over me, just like a big, cozy blanket. As I rest in the safe haven of Your love, I pray You'll fill me with joy and gladness. It's easy to rejoice in You because You've done so many wonderful things for me. You love me unconditionally. You've given me mercy that I don't deserve. And because of that, I love to sing to You! Even when I've had a rough day, I pray my songs to You will be filled with joy and thankfulness because You are good to me. I love You, Lord! Amen.

BECAUSE GOD PROTECTS ME,
I CAN REJOICE AND BE GLAD!

I DON'T HAVE TO BE AFRAID

*See, God saves me. I will trust and
not be afraid. For the Lord God is
my strength and song. And He has
become the One Who saves me.*

ISAIAH 12:2 NLV

Lord God, thank You for saving me! Thank You
for sending Jesus to this earth so that He could be
my rescuer. Thank You that I am saved through
Him. It's such an amazing relief to know I don't
have to be afraid! I put my complete trust in
You. You are my strength. In fact, Your power is
only made stronger when I'm weak. You are the
song that I sing early in the morning and late at
night. You are the only One who saves me. When
I trust in You, You replace my fear with peace.
I praise You for that wonderful peace that only
comes from You. And I praise You for Your love
and all the kindness You've shown me. In Jesus'
saving name I pray, amen.

I DON'T HAVE TO BE AFRAID
BECAUSE GOD SAVES ME!

THERE IS ONE

*There is one God. There is one Man standing
between God and men. That Man is Christ
Jesus. He gave His life for all men so they
could go free and not be held by the
power of sin. God made this known
to the world at the right time.*
1 TIMOTHY 2:5–6 NLV

Father, I'm so glad You've made a way to Yourself!
I could never get to You on my own. I couldn't do
enough good things. My imperfections and sins
separate me from You, but You made a way for
me through Jesus. You sent Jesus to bridge the
gap between You and me. He even gave His own
life so I could get to You. That is pretty awesome
and absolutely amazing. It's also pretty humbling
because I feel like I really don't deserve that. But
because of Jesus and His death, I can be free! I'm
not held by the power of sin anymore. And You
didn't keep that freedom a secret. Thank You!
Thank You for making a way to You! In Jesus'
name I pray, amen.

THERE IS ONE BRIDGE BETWEEN ME
AND GOD. THAT BRIDGE IS JESUS!

YOU CARE!

Answer me when I call, O my God
Who is right and good! You have made
a way for me when I needed help.
Be kind to me, and hear my prayer.

PSALM 4:1 NLV

God, You are right and good! Thank You for making a way for me. When I need help, You're there. When I call out to You, You answer. When I pray, You hear what I say. And You are oh so very kind to me. When I think of all You do for me and how You treat me, I know I matter to You. You pay attention to what I say and do, and You don't only pay attention, You respond to what's going on. You answer me. You make a way. I don't have to worry about what could possibly happen because You're there. Please help me live with a greater trust and more gratefulness for You. In Jesus' name I pray, amen.

GOD IS SO CARING AND KIND!
HE LISTENS TO ME AND HELPS ME.

WHO DO I THINK I AM?

Do not be wise in your own eyes;
Fear the LORD and turn away from evil.
PROVERBS 3:7 NASB

Lord, I admit that I think better of myself than I should. Even though I have days when I'm pretty critical of myself, I'm still proud. I'm wise in my own eyes and I think I know better than other people. But I really should have a more realistic view of myself. I need to fear You instead of trusting in myself. I need to respect You instead of basing everything on my own opinions. And Father, when I notice evil in the world—or even choices throughout my day that would push me farther away from You and Your will—I pray I'll turn away from it. I want to turn toward You instead. I want to please You with what I say and think and do, Father, even when that seems difficult. Please help me! In Jesus' name I pray, amen.

I NEED TO TURN AWAY FROM
MY OWN PRIDE AND DESIRES.

SET APART

Know that the L<small>ORD</small> has set apart
his faithful servant for himself;
the L<small>ORD</small> hears when I call to him.
PSALM 4:3 NIV

Lord, I love You so much! I love to serve You. As I look for ways to follow the way You lead me, help me remember one important fact: You've set me apart! As I serve You, I can remember that You've prepared me for the good things I can do. You'll give me work to do and the abilities I'll need to do it. Please help me rely on Your strength to keep serving You even when I'm afraid. When I feel like I'm not ready to do what You call me to do, please fill me with Your Spirit and work through me. When I call to You for help, wisdom, or the right words, please help me remember that You hear. Just as You've set me apart for Your work, You'll also direct the way I serve You. That's a huge relief! I don't have to have everything figured out in advance; I just need to trust You moment by moment. Amen.

THE LORD HAS SET ME
APART TO SERVE HIM!

KNOWING AND LOOKING

Those who know Your name will put their trust in You. For You, O Lord, have never left alone those who look for You.

PSALM 9:10 NLV

O Lord, I love the way that You'll never leave me alone when I look for You! I love to see You in the big picture and little details of every day. As I watch You at work in my life, my trust in You grows. Not only do I know Your name, but I know You. As I get to know You more, I love You more. You're like a best friend I want to know everything about. And the more I know and love You, the more I trust You too. I know You're working details out for Your will, and I know if I'm trusting in You and looking for You, I'll be right in the middle of Your will. Thanks that I don't have to go through my life alone! Life really is so much better shared with You. I love You!

WHEN I KNOW GOD AND LOOK FOR HIM IN MY LIFE, I TRUST HIM MORE.

PEACE LIKE A RIVER

If only you had paid attention to my commands, your peace would have been like a river, your well-being like the waves of the sea.
ISAIAH 48:18 NIV

Father God, You've promised me peace when I pay attention to You and Your commands. When I try to live life my own way, one thing always happens: my peace disappears. I doubt I make the right choice. I obsess over what I could do differently. I question what I'm thinking and feeling. But when I choose to listen to You and live the way You say I should, I don't have to stress. I can feel at peace. The trick, though, is finding what You command. And Your commands are found in the Bible. The more time I spend reading and studying and praying about what Your Word says, the more clarity and peace I'll experience. In fact, Your peace will flow through me, just like a river. And Your comfort will wash over me like the waves of the ocean. Thanks for that peace! It only comes through You. In Your name I pray, amen.

WHEN I PAY ATTENTION TO GOD'S
COMMANDS, I'LL EXPERIENCE PEACE.

LICHTEN MY DARKNESS

For it is you who light my lamp;
the Lord my God lightens my darkness.
PSALM 18:28 ESV

Lord my God, sometimes it feels like there's a lot of darkness in my days. I'm either confused and unsure of what I should do, or I see so much going wrong in the world around me. It's easy to get scared. And it's even easier to obsess over what is wrong. Instead of focusing on the darkness, though, please help me to see all of the ways You lighten my darkness. Jesus said that He is the light of the world. Whoever follows Him won't need to walk in darkness, but have the light of life instead. I don't want to walk in darkness. I'm glad that Jesus is the light and that You sent Him to light my way. I pray I'll walk in the freedom and clarity Your light brings. And I pray I'll shine Your light in the darkness around me! In Jesus' name I pray, amen.

GOD LIGHTENS MY DARKNESS.

CONTENTMENT

A God-like life gives us much when we
are happy for what we have. We came
into this world with nothing. For sure,
when we die, we will take nothing with us.
1 TIMOTHY 6:6–7 NLV

Father, contentment seems like such a strange concept in today's world. Do I know many people who are happy with what they have? Am I satisfied with my belongings? Advertisers are always trying to get me to buy the next thing. And I find myself thinking a lot about what I'd love to buy or have. But I can be happy with what I already have! I have so much through You. And just like I came into this world without anything, You've provided all I truly need. When I die, I can't take any of my stuff with me. Not clothing, not electronics, not even my favorite childhood toy. Since my belongings are just things that can get ruined, please help me remember they won't last forever. And please help me be happier with what I already have. In Jesus' name I pray, amen.

I CAN BE HAPPY WITH WHAT I HAVE!

HE HAS HEARD

*Praise be to the Lord, for he
has heard my cry for mercy.*

PSALM 28:6 NIV

Lord, I've just come out of a really difficult time.
You know how much I've faced. You know I feel
like I've come to the end of my rope. I reached
the point when I couldn't rely on myself any
more. I needed You. And I needed Your mercy.
I praise You because You are good! Even in my
nightmare situation, You rescued me! Even when
I doubted I could go on, You faithfully stayed by
my side and led my way. Without You, I don't
know what I would have done. Thank You for
Your love. Thank You for Your mercy. I praise You
for listening to me and answering my prayers.
Thank You for never letting me go. In Jesus'
name I pray, amen.

IN MY TOUGHEST MOMENTS,
GOD HEARS MY CRIES FOR MERCY.

PEOPLE PLEASER

*Am I now trying to win the approval of human
beings, or of God? Or am I trying to please
people? If I were still trying to please people,
I would not be a servant of Christ.*

GALATIANS 1:10 NIV

Father God, I love You. Please help me remember that Your approval is all that matters. A lot of days, it's really tempting to try to win the approval of someone else—maybe my friends, girls I wish would be my friends, someone I really like, my teachers, or parents. But no matter what any of those people think, You are the One who matters, Lord. You are the One I need to please. I truly want to be a servant of Christ. When I start feeling pressured by what other people do or ask, please help me focus on pleasing You instead of anyone else. In Jesus' name I pray, amen.

I WANT TO WIN THE APPROVAL
OF GOD, NOT HUMANS.

HOW LONG?

How long, O Lord? Will You forget me forever?
How long will You hide Your face from me?
How long must I plan what to do in my soul,
and have sorrow in my heart all the day?
How long will those who hate me rise above me?
PSALM 13:1–2 NLV

Lord, are You there? I trust that You are! But sometimes, it doesn't seem like You're listening. And sometimes it even feels like You've forgotten about me. But I'm here! And I need You! I long for Your guidance. When I feel unsure about Your will for my life, I try to figure things out on my own. But trying to make choices on my own doesn't always end up for the best. I don't want to live with sorrow or regret. Please guide me! Show me what You'd like me to do. I'm trying to patiently wait for You. Please lead me! Amen.

EVEN IF IT SEEMS LIKE GOD HAS
FORGOTTEN ME, HE HASN'T.

GUARD MY HEART

Above all else, guard your heart,
for everything you do flows from it.
PROVERBS 4:23 NIV

Father, thank You for creating me! I praise You that You loved me so much to make me in a wonderful way. You created me so that everything would flow from my heart. My feelings are powerful and reveal a lot about what I'm thinking. Because of that, I pray I'll protect my heart. Things of this world have a way of sneaking in and invading my thoughts. It's easy to obsess over people or thoughts or things. When I let that happen, I let my guard down. I pray I'll be wise about what I think about. In fact, like 2 Corinthians 10:5 says, I should "take every thought captive to make it obedient to Christ." As I really examine my thoughts, I'll be able to guard my heart better. I really need Your help to do this though. In Jesus' name I pray, amen.

I NEED TO GUARD MY
HEART AND THOUGHTS!

LIFE, JOY, AND PLEASURES

You will make known to me the way of life; In Your presence is fullness of joy; In Your right hand there are pleasures forever.
PSALM 16:11 NASB

My Lord and my God, I am so glad I know You! Whenever I'm in Your presence I'm filled with joy. The worries of this world can't drag me down when my eyes and my mind are set on You. I've tried finding joy in my own way, but never truly find it without You. You continue to make known to me the way of life. As long as I follow You, I know that I'll always experience life and pleasures. That's forever life! And forever pleasures! Because I know You, I don't have to be afraid. I can rest in Your promises and know You'll love and guide me. You'll also fill my life with good things. I love you, Lord! In Jesus' name I pray, amen.

THROUGH THE LORD, MY LIFE WILL
BE FILLED WITH JOY AND PLEASURES.

NO FEAR

For God gave us a spirit not of fear but
of power and love and self-control.
2 TIMOTHY 1:7 ESV

Father God, I don't always feel brave. In fact, sometimes it's really easy to feel scared. But I need to remember that I don't need to be afraid. In fact, that spirit of fear that I feel isn't from You. What You have given me is so much better. You've given me a spirit of power! And love! And self-control. The next time I feel fear creeping in, please remind me what You have given me. I pray I'll boldly use Your power. I pray Your love will shine in my life. And I pray I'll be self-controlled enough to step out in faith and do what I should—not cower in fear. Thank You for generously giving me power, love, and self-control. All are really good gifts. In Jesus' name I pray, amen.

I DON'T HAVE TO BE AFRAID! GOD'S GIVEN
ME A SPIRIT OF POWER, LOVE,
AND SELF-CONTROL.

WHEN I CALL YOU WILL ANSWER

I have called to You, O God, for You will answer me. Listen to me and hear my words.

PSALM 17:6 NLV

My Lord, I love that I can trust You and know You care about me! In fact, You care so much that when I call to You, You listen. You hear my words. And it's not like You hear what I say but are tuning me out. No, You actually listen and pay attention to what I'm saying and how I'm feeling. It's not even like what I say goes to voicemail and You get back to me whenever You feel like it. No, You pay attention every moment and You answer me. I'm so thankful You are a God who hears and knows—not just everything going on in the world, but You specifically pay attention to me too. It's so amazing to remember that I matter to You! I love You, Lord!

WHEN I CALL TO GOD,
HE LISTENS AND ANSWERS.

HIGHER

"For My thoughts are not your thoughts,
and My ways are not your ways," says the
Lord. "For as the heavens are higher than
the earth, so are My ways higher than your
ways, and My thoughts than your thoughts."
ISAIAH 55:8–9 NLV

Father God, sometimes I like to think that I know it all, even though in reality I'm kind of clueless about a lot of things. But You do know it all. And Your thoughts are different from mine. The ways You work are different from my ways too. In fact, everything You think and do is so much higher than I can even comprehend. Because of that, I pray I'll trust You more. You have a marvelous plan, even when some things that happen seem awful. Instead of focusing on how I'm not getting my way, I pray I'll remember that You're in control. You have a plan. And as You put Your plans into motion, I just need to trust You. In Jesus' name I pray, amen.

GOD'S WAYS ARE NOT MY WAYS!

THE LORD IS MY STRENGTH

I love You, O LORD, my strength.
PSALM 18:1 ESV

O Lord, when I think of worldly strength, I think of athletes who train to become stronger. Strength training isn't easy. In fact, it takes a lot of time and slowly builds over time. When someone begins strength training, they can't lift fifty pounds right away. No, they start with ten-pound weights, and over time they increase what they can lift. As their muscles get stronger, they can lift more and more. I love that, spiritually speaking, You're my strength, Lord! But just like weight-lifting, I can't expect to instantly have amazing faith and strength. I need to exercise my faith in You. I need to trust You more and more. I need to watch You work in my life more and more. As I do, Your strength will grow and build in me. You'll be able to work in amazing ways, but I need to start small and patiently exercise my faith in You. I love You!

THE LORD IS MY STRENGTH.
THE MORE I TRUST HIM, THE MORE
HIS STRENGTH GROWS IN ME.

LIKE A TREE

As you have put your trust in Christ Jesus
the Lord to save you from the punishment of
sin, now let Him lead you in every step. Have
your roots planted deep in Christ. Grow in
Him. Get your strength from Him. Let Him
make you strong in the faith as you have been
taught. Your life should be full of thanks to Him.
COLOSSIANS 2:6–7 NLV

Lord Jesus, I'm so glad I've put my trust in You.
You are the Lord of my life. I trust You to save
me from the punishment of my sin. While Your
saving grace completely changes my future, I
pray I'll trust You for the rest of my life. Please
lead me in every step of every day. I want to
plant the roots of my life deep in You. I don't
want shallow roots that can wither easily or get
yanked out and destroyed like a delicate seed-
ling. Instead, I want to be like an established tree
with deep roots in You and plenty of beautiful
growth. I want to draw my strength from You,
through faith and obedience. I want to bear Your
fruit in my life. In Your name I pray, amen.

I NEED TO PLANT THE ROOTS OF MY
LIFE IN CHRIST AND GROW IN HIM.

HELP!

In my distress I called to the Lord; I cried to my God for help. From his temple he heard my voice; my cry came before him, into his ears.
PSALM 18:6 NIV

Father! Please help me! Something so unexpected and so completely out of my control has happened. I don't know what to do. I feel helpless, and I have no idea what will happen. But I do know I can cry out to You for help and mercy. I know You hear me. You know what's going on. I pray You'll quiet my heart and give me peace. Please help me trust You completely. I pray I'll rest and trust in You alone. I pray I'll glorify You in this situation. Help me shine for You even when things seem so dark and uncertain. I love You and I'm thankful I can trust in You! In Jesus' name I pray, amen.

WHEN I NEED HELP,
I CAN CRY OUT TO GOD!

A STRONG PLACE

The way of the Lord is a strong-place
to those who are faithful, but it
destroys those who do wrong.
PROVERBS 10:29 NLV

Lord, Your way isn't always easy or comfortable.
Especially in situations I face with my friends, it
can be really hard to stand up for You and Your
truth. But Your way is right. And it's a strong
place. It's what I want to follow. Even if and
when it's difficult, I pray I'll stay close to You
and follow Your will and Your way. I want to
do right. I want to live by faith in You. I want
to live a life of love that overflows to everyone
around me. I want a thriving life that's right in
Your eyes. I don't want to do what's wrong. I
don't want to disobey and be destroyed. I love
You! And I want to be faithful to You forever. In
Jesus' name I pray, amen.

WHEN I AM FAITHFUL, THE LORD'S
WAY IS A STRONG PLACE FOR ME.

WHERE ARE YOU?

Why do You stand far away, Lord? Why do
You hide Yourself in times of trouble?
PSALM 10:1 NASB

O Lord, I know You're there. I know You can hear me. But sometimes it just doesn't feel like it. I can't sense You near. When bad things happen, I wonder why. Are you going to step in and make things right? Can I trust Your will even when things seem awful in my life and in the world? I could really use Your help. When I can't feel You near and when it doesn't seem like You care about my situation, please reassure me of Your love. Please open my eyes to see the little ways You're working. When I'm in trouble and it feels like You're hiding, please gently guide me. I want to experience Your power and peace working in my life. You seem so distant, but I know You're not. Please comfort me in the way only You can. Please help me experience peace and hope as I choose to put my trust in You. In Jesus' name I pray, amen.

SOMETIMES IT FEELS LIKE
GOD IS HIDING. BUT HE IS THERE.

TAKEN CAPTIVE?

*See to it that there is no one who takes
you captive through philosophy and
empty deception, in accordance with
human tradition, in accordance with
the elementary principles of the world,
rather than in accordance with Christ.*

COLOSSIANS 2:8 NASB

Father God, there's so much in this world that
goes against Your Word. So many beliefs and
teachings don't honor You. When I hear what
some people say, I know they're persuasive.
And deceptive. It's easy to get caught up in what
thoughts are popular right now. But I don't want
those lies to take me captive. I don't want to be
deceived! Please help me read and learn and
know Your truth. Please help me apply it to my
life and any situation that comes my way. And
please bring clarity to situations so I'll be able
to discern what is Your truth and what is a
worldly lie. I want to follow Christ! In His name
I pray, amen.

**THE BELIEFS AND TRADITIONS OF THIS
WORLD ARE DIFFERENT THAN GOD'S TRUTH.**

SAVING POWER

*Now I know that the Lord saves His chosen
one. He will answer him from His holy heaven,
with the saving power of His right hand.*

PSALM 20:6 NLV

Lord, I'm not sure why You've chosen me, but
I'm so thankful You have. It doesn't really matter
if I understand Your choice. But I do know how
very grateful I am that You've chosen to save me
through Jesus. And You answer me from Your
holy heaven. You have the power to save—and
in Your perfection You have every right to choose
not to save at all. Yet You decided I was worth
saving. Thank You that Your choice to save me is
started by You and accomplished through Jesus.
I believe He is the risen Lord. I believe You raised
Him from the dead. I believe You have the power
to save me from death. You have saving power,
and I know my eternity rests on that. In Jesus'
powerful name I pray, amen.

THE LORD HAS THE POWER TO SAVE.

WHERE'S MY TREASURE?

*For where your treasure is,
there your heart will be also.*
MATTHEW 6:21 NIV

Father, it's easy to see that I really value the things I set my heart on. In fact, I could consider those things my treasure. I'm tempted to treasure other people, my accomplishments, my success, certain relationships, clothes, belongings, money, my looks, popularity, fun experiences, and hopes for the future. When I treasure those things, I end up setting my heart on them. I pray that I'll start to set my heart on You. I want to find treasure in knowing, loving, and trusting You more. I don't want to store up treasures here on earth. Not only are they short-lived, but they'll also get destroyed really easily. I want to store up my treasures in heaven where no one can steal them and nothing can destroy them. Please help me find great joy in You as I set my heart on You. In Jesus' name I pray, amen.

WHEN I STORE UP MY TREASURE IN HEAVEN,
MY HEART WILL BE THERE TOO.

STRONG AND COURAGEOUS

Be strong and take heart,
all you who hope in the Lord.
PSALM 31:24 NIV

Lord, I trust and hope in You. In fact, You're the One I count on. I believe what You promise, and I take You at Your Word. While that brings me a lot of comfort and peace, I get some other great benefits too, like strength! I can be strong because I hope in You. My heart can take courage too. That's a huge relief, because when I face difficult things and I'm tempted to feel scared or worried, I can be courageous instead. Strength and courage aren't easily found on my own, but because of my hope in You, they almost become my superpowers. Thanks for filling my heart with so much more than what I have on my own. Amen.

WHEN I HOPE IN THE LORD, HE WILL
FILL ME WITH STRENGTH AND COURAGE.

FREEDOM!

Christian brother, you were chosen to be free.
Be careful that you do not please your old
selves by sinning because you are free.
Live this free life by loving and helping others.
GALATIANS 5:13 NLV

Lord Jesus, thank You for setting me free! Your law of the Spirit of life has freed me from the law of sin and death! And while the freedom You've given me is beyond amazing, it's also pretty mind-blowing to know that You've chosen me too. I pray I won't abuse my freedom in You by sinning. You've given me forgiveness, but I don't want to run wild with sinful choices just because I might feel like I can get away with it. No, I want to appreciate the forgiveness You give. I want to use Your freedom in a really good way. In fact, I'd love to use my freedom by helping other people and loving them really, really well. I want to use the freedom I have in You to do Your work in this world. In Your name I pray, amen.

I CAN USE MY FREEDOM IN CHRIST
TO LOVE AND HELP OTHERS.

FILLED

For our heart is full of joy in Him,
because we trust in His holy name.
O Lord, let Your loving-kindness be
upon us as we put our hope in You.
PSALM 33:21–22 NLV

O Lord, I put my hope in You! It's amazing that when I do that, You repay me with so much more love and kindness than I could ever ask for or deserve. And when I trust in You and Your holy name, You fill my heart with joy! Not just a passing happiness, but amazing joy. You fill me with joy, love, and kindness that's nothing like I could get on my own, and like nothing the world has to offer. Even though I can't describe how wonderful it is, I'm still grateful for it. So thank You! Thanks for filling my life with so many incredible things and for being someone completely worthy of my trust and hope. In Jesus' name I pray, amen.

WHEN I TRUST IN GOD, HE FILLS ME
WITH JOY. WHEN I PUT MY HOPE IN HIM,
HE FILLS ME WITH HIS LOVE.

RIGHT OR WRONG

The one who is right with God is kept from trouble, but the sinful get into trouble instead.
PROVERBS 11:8 NLV

Father, there's a right way to live—and a wrong way. Sometimes it's hard to recognize what's truly right or wrong. In fact, a lot of decisions I make seem to be in more of a gray area. There are some good things and bad things all mixed together, but nothing seems completely right or completely wrong. Even when I don't think the choices are completely sinful, I need to remember that some decisions honor You more. And other decisions don't honor You but seem really, really appealing. If I get right down to it, it's easy for me to justify some of my sins. They seem like they could be the better choice, just because they might make my life better for the moment. Please clearly show me what's right and wrong. And please remind me that choosing the right way is what You want. Your right way will keep me from trouble. Amen.

I ALWAYS HAVE A CHOICE TO DO WHAT'S RIGHT OR WHAT'S WRONG. CHOOSING THE RIGHT WAY WILL KEEP ME FROM TROUBLE.

MERCY!

Hear my cry for mercy as
I call to you for help.
PSALM 28:2 NIV

Mercy, Lord! I call out to You for mercy. I need Your help. I need You to step into my situations and make things right. Things feel completely out of my control. I'm scared; I don't know what to do, and I know I don't have the answers. But You do. You are in control. In You, I don't have to fear. You do have the answers. And through You, You can reveal what I should do. I pray You'll work in a wonderful way. Please make things right. Please help me trust You more and more as You walk with me through this challenge. I pray I'll spy Your mercy all around me. And I pray I'll notice the surprising ways You send Your help. I'm putting my trust completely in You! I know You can and will redeem this situation. In Jesus' name I pray, amen.

I CAN CRY TO GOD FOR
MERCY AND FOR HELP.

WHAT I CAN DO

Wash yourselves. Make yourselves clean.
Take your sinful actions from My eyes. Stop
doing sinful things. Learn to do good. Look for
what is right and fair. Speak strong words to
those who make it hard for people. Stand up
for the rights of those who have no parents.
Help the woman whose husband has died.
ISAIAH 1:16–17 NLV

Father, sometimes I wonder what I should do. I'm
glad Your Word is filled with direction! I want to
live it out. Like You've instructed, I need to stop
doing sinful things. I need to learn to do good.
I may not always know how, but I can learn. I
also can start looking for what is right in this
world. I need to treat all people fairly and I need
to stand up for people who are treated poorly.
When people are mean or unfair or unkind, I
need to speak up for what's right. And I need
to help orphans and widows when God brings
them into my life. Please help me! Amen.

I NEED TO STOP SINNING, LEARN TO
DO GOOD, WORK AGAINST INJUSTICE,
AND HELP THE HELPLESS.

I WILL TELL YOU

I told my sin to You. I did not hide my wrong-doing. I said, "I will tell my sins to the Lord." And You forgave the guilt of my sin.

PSALM 32:5 NLV

Father, I can come to You with anything. I don't have to be afraid to tell You what I'm thinking or even confess what I've done—You already know. It's tempting to try to hide what I've done wrong. But I don't have to hide. I don't have to live a life of deception. I can tell You my sins. And when I tell You, You'll forgive me of my guilt. That's pretty amazing because I'm feeling really guilty over the things I've done wrong. I'm sorry that I sinned. I wish I could have a do-over. I know I'll need to live with the consequences of my sin here on earth, but I'm so thankful for Your forgiveness. I'm thankful You gave me a new start. I'm so thankful for the way You took away my guilt. Thank You! In Jesus' name I pray, amen.

WHEN I TELL MY SINS TO THE LORD,
HE'LL FORGIVE ME AND TAKE AWAY MY GUILT.

NO WORRIES!

"So do not worry about tomorrow;
for tomorrow will worry about itself.
Each day has enough trouble of its own."
MATTHEW 6:34 NASB

Father God, I'm so thankful I don't have to worry about tomorrow! Am I still tempted to worry? Of course. Is it easier to obsess over what might or might not happen instead of trusting You'll work everything out? Unfortunately, yes. But even if I'm inclined to worry about the future, I pray I won't. Instead, I want to show how much I trust You by living by faith—and living without fear. Please help me focus on the opportunities and challenges You've given me today. I want to work through whatever I'm facing today. And I want to glorify You with what I choose to do or say. When I feel tempted to dwell on what might happen in the future, please help me look around and see what's actually here in the present. In Jesus' name I pray, amen.

I DON'T HAVE TO WORRY ABOUT WHAT
MIGHT HAPPEN TOMORROW! INSTEAD,
I NEED TO FOCUS ON TODAY.

MY SAFE PLACE

O Lord, in You I have found a safe place.
Let me never be ashamed. Set me free,
because You do what is right and good.
PSALM 31:1 NLV

O Lord, You are my safe place. In You, I don't have to fear what might happen. I don't even have to fear what actually is happening. Even if everything in this earth falls away, You'll never fall away, Lord. You are real. You are true. You last forever. Because of who You are, I pray I'll live in confidence and boldness. Please help me live for You without any shame. I want to follow You, feeling completely safe as I'm in the middle of Your will. Instead of feeling trapped by the chains of worry or guilt or shame, I pray I'll live in freedom that comes through Christ alone. Because You do what is right and good, I can trust that You'll do what's ultimately right and good in my life. I love You and trust You! In Jesus' name I pray, amen.

I HAVE FOUND A SAFE
PLACE IN THE LORD.

WHAT IS RIGHT

Turn away from the sinful things young people want to do. Go after what is right. Have a desire for faith and love and peace. Do this with those who pray to God from a clean heart.

2 TIMOTHY 2:22 NLV

Father God, it's really easy to try to go after what seems attractive and appealing. It's so hard to step back and think about possible consequences of my decisions. Even if I know something is wrong, sometimes I still choose to do that wrong thing! I don't want that though. I don't want to make big mistakes. And I don't want to sin against You. Even if young people have a tendency to do sinful things, I pray I'll be different. I really want to go after what is right and make good choices. Please help my faith in You grow. I want to love others like You've loved me. And as I do that, I pray You'll fill my heart with Your peace. Please protect me from sinful choices. Give me clean hands and a pure heart. I love You!

I WANT TO TURN AWAY FROM SINFUL THINGS AND GO AFTER WHAT IS RIGHT.

COME TO MY RESCUE

Turn your ear to me, come quickly to
my rescue; be my rock of refuge,
a strong fortress to save me.
PSALM 31:2 NIV

Lord! Please help me! I pray You'll listen to my prayer and rescue me quickly. I feel like I might be in so much trouble right now. You know what's going on in my heart. And You know what circumstances I'm facing. Please help! I don't want to be afraid. Instead, I want to rest on Your promises. You can be my rock of refuge. You can be my strong fortress. I pray You'll save me! Please save me from my situation right now. Through Jesus, I pray You'll save me for an eternity spent with You. I pray Your saving power will show through my weakness even right now. Please fill me with Your peace. I trust You! And when I feel like my faith is failing, please help my lack of faith. In Jesus' strong name I pray, amen.

THE LORD CAN BE MY STRONG FORTRESS AND ROCK OF REFUGE WHEN I'M IN TROUBLE.

WHAT LASTS?

Charm is deceptive, and beauty
is fleeting; but a woman who
fears the LORD is to be praised.
PROVERBS 31:30 NIV

Father, so often I focus on the way I look. I find
myself obsessing over the things I wear or some
of my features—my hair, my eyes, my smile,
even my fingers or toes! I spend so much time
concentrating on what I look like that I don't
even stop to consider what's on my inside. What
is my relationship with You like? How much do
I fear and love You? The two—my looks and my
relationship with You—seem like they shouldn't
be related. But only one of the two will last. My
beauty will fade, no matter how hard I try. But
my relationship with You? It will last forever.
And the closer I am to You, the more beautiful
You'll make me from the inside out. Your love
and beauty will have a way of radiating out of
me to the people around me. Thank You for Your
beauty! In Jesus' name I pray, amen.

BEAUTY DOESN'T LAST,
BUT MY RELATIONSHIP WITH
THE LORD LASTS FOREVER.

FILLED WITH JOY!

I will be glad and full of joy in
Your loving-kindness. For You
have seen my suffering. You have
known the troubles of my soul.
PSALM 31:7 NLV

Lord, Your love is so wonderful! Feeling Your love
and knowing You love me fills me with joy and
gladness. I don't have to be happy all the time,
but deep down, I have a joy that all the troubles
of this world can't take away. Even when I suffer, You know what I'm going through. When
I'm in trouble or feel so upset, You know what
I'm feeling. And You love me anyway. When I'm
feeling really down, I pray Your love will comfort
me. I'd love to find joy through Your love even
during my saddest days. Thank You for seeing
and knowing me. And thank You for loving me.
In Jesus' name I pray, amen.

GOD SEES AND KNOWS MY STRUGGLES,
AND HE FILLS ME WITH HIS LOVE AND JOY.

KEEP DOING GOOD!

*Do not let yourselves get tired of doing good.
If we do not give up, we will get what is
coming to us at the right time.*
GALATIANS 6:9 NLV

Father, sometimes I get so tired out. It feels like I'm working and working and working, and after all that hard work, I get tired. I don't just feel that way with schoolwork and other activities, but I feel that way about doing good too. I really want to do good. But it's hard to do good all the time. Sometimes I feel selfish and would rather have people do good to me. Other times, I'd rather treat people the way they treat me, but I know I should treat them the way I'd like to be treated. You've asked me to shine Your light to the world and be known for my love. I pray I won't give up and that I won't give up if and when I get tired. Please give me tenacity and grit to keep doing good, no matter what. In Jesus' name I pray, amen.

DON'T GIVE UP! I NEED TO KEEP
DOING GOOD, EVEN IF I GET TIRED.

AMAZING LOVE

How great is Your loving-kindness!
You have stored it up for those who
fear You. You show it to those who
trust in You in front of the sons of men.
PSALM 31:19 NLV

Oh Lord, You are so good! Your kindness is amazing. And Your love? You've actually stored it up just for those who fear You. The thing is, You don't pour out Your love on just anyone. You store it up and show it to people who have a relationship with You. When I recognize You for who You are—the God of the universe! Maker of heaven and earth!—I have so much respect for You and a healthy fear of You. I stand in awe of You! Through my awe and respect, I trust You more and more, because I know You're at work in the world and in my life. And as my fear of You and trust in You grows, You shower me with Your kindness and love. You are so good to me! Thank You!

WHEN I FEAR THE LORD AND TRUST HIM MORE,
HE WILL SHOW ME THE AMAZING LOVE
HE'S STORED UP FOR ME.

WHAT DO I SEEK?

If then you have been raised with Christ,
seek the things that are above, where
Christ is, seated at the right hand of God.
COLOSSIANS 3:1 ESV

Father, I love You and thank You for the gift of Jesus. I trust Him as my Lord and do believe He died, rose again, and is alive today! I also believe He has saved me from my sins. I trust in Him and believe I'm also raised with Him. I don't have to fear death or anything in this world. I'd like to live out my belief. Because I don't have to fear anything in this world, I want to start seeking things that are above—things that matter for an eternity. Please help me discern what issues matter for an eternity and what things are fleeting. I pray I'll live with a different perspective than others around me. I want to courageously live to please You and You alone—not other people around me, and not even myself. I love You!

IF I BELIEVE IN CHRIST, I NEED TO
SEEK THINGS THAT ARE ABOVE—
NOT EARTHLY THINGS.

TEARS ON MY PILLOW

O my God, I cry during the day,
but You do not answer. I cry during
the night, but I find no rest.

PSALM 22:2 NLV

Lord, I've been feeling so emotional lately. It seems like I'm getting upset very easily, and so many things in life are bringing me down. I've even been crying a lot. And even when I cry to You, I don't feel comfort. Where are You? When I get upset, it doesn't seem like You're answering me. And at night, if I cry myself to sleep, I don't feel at peace. It's like I can't feel truly rested. You've promised me peace though. I pray I'll continue to trust You, even when I can't sense You near me. I pray You'll guide me as I make choices, even when it doesn't feel like You're near. I want my life to reflect my love for You. And I want to keep loving You, even when it feels like You've left me all by myself. Your Word promises that You are always with me. Please reveal Yourself to me! I want to know You're near! Amen.

EVEN WHEN IT SEEMS GOD ISN'T
NEAR ME, I CAN KEEP CRYING OUT
TO HIM. AND I TRUST THAT HE IS NEAR.

GOOD TREATMENT

*So whatever you wish that others
would do to you, do also to them.*
MATTHEW 7:12 ESV

Father, it's hard for me to remember to treat others the way I'd like to be treated. So often I'd rather treat people the way they treat me: If they're kind to me, I'll treat them with kindness and favor. But if they're mean? I could be mean right back. If they hurt my feelings, it would seem like a good payback to hurt their feelings too. But You don't ask me to do that. In fact, You tell me not to do that. You ask me not to react to the way people treat me. It doesn't matter what they say or do to me—anything and everything I do needs to be just as I'd want someone to treat me. I really do need to treat people the way I'd like to be treated, and that's with plenty of kindness and respect. It's hard to do this all the time though. Could You please help me? In Jesus' name I pray, amen.

I NEED TO TREAT OTHER PEOPLE
THE WAY I'D LIKE TO BE TREATED.

HE SEES AND UNDERSTANDS

The Lord looks from heaven. He sees
all the sons of men. From where He sits
He looks upon all who live on the earth.
He made the hearts of them all. And He
understands whatever they do.
PSALM 33:13–15 NLV

Lord, You are so amazing! You know all. You are everywhere all the time. You created every single person on this planet and You see and know each one of us. I don't even totally understand everything I do, but You do! You know me even better than I know myself. Since nothing I say or do could ever surprise You, help me remember I can come to You with absolutely anything. You already know my deepest, darkest thoughts. You know my struggles and insecurities. And You know all of my favorite things because You created me to appreciate them. I'm in awe of You and I worship You for who You are. In Jesus' name I pray, amen.

THE LORD CREATED ABSOLUTELY
EVERYONE, AND HE SEES AND
UNDERSTANDS WHAT EVERYONE DOES.

BE HAPPY!

You who are young, be happy while you are young, and let your heart give you joy in the days of your youth. Follow the ways of your heart and whatever your eyes see, but know that for all these things God will bring you into judgment.
ECCLESIASTES 11:9 NIV

Father, I pray I'll enjoy this time of my life for what it is: special. I only get to be young once; please help me make the most of it! I need to remember that the choices I make right now have consequences—and some of those consequences could last the rest of my life. Please help me balance having fun and making wise choices that won't bring shame or embarrassment. I don't want to spend my teenage years making wild choices—just choices that bring a lot of happiness and joy. I want to listen to Your Holy Spirit's guidance. Please prick my conscience when I shouldn't do something, yet enjoy times that are pleasing to You. I'm trusting You to guide me! Amen.

NOW'S THE PERFECT TIME TO HAVE FUN!
BUT I NEED TO REMEMBER I'LL HAVE TO
GIVE AN ANSWER FOR ALL I CHOOSE TO DO.

THE WATER'S RISING

Therefore let all the faithful pray to you while you may be found; surely the rising of the mighty waters will not reach them.

PSALM 32:6 NIV

Almighty God, things feel like they're completely out of my control right now. But if I stop to think about it, things never are in my control. That reality and lack of control scares me. I don't want to live a life of fear, though. Even if it seems like life's mighty waters are rushing and rising, You are the One in control. I release my fears to You, Father. Please fill me with Your peace. As I'm stressed out over what might happen or even what is happening, I will keep praying to You and honestly telling You what I'm thinking and feeling. Even if everything else is taken away from me, You'll never leave me. You'll never forsake me. And because of that, I don't have to fear. Thank You for Your peace! Amen.

EVEN IN THE MIDDLE OF STRESSFUL, UNCERTAIN SITUATIONS, GOD IS IN CONTROL. I CAN TELL HIM EXACTLY WHAT I'M FEELING AND THINKING.

A GOOD WORK

*I am sure that God Who began the good
work in you will keep on working in you
until the day Jesus Christ comes again.*
PHILIPPIANS 1:6 NLV

Father, it's amazing to know You have begun a
good work in me! You've chosen me. You have
already prepared good works for me to do. You
started a really good work in my life, and You're
going to keep working in me and my life. Thank
You! I pray I'll be open and willing to follow Your
lead. I trust that You'll guide me and show me
what You'd have me do. When I'm confused,
please give me clarity. When I need to make a
decision, please guide me in the choice that will
honor You the most. I pray You'll use all the gifts
and strengths You've given me to work out the
good things You have planned for me. I'm glad
I can trust You! I can't wait to see what You'll do
in my life! In Jesus' name I pray, amen.

GOD STARTED A GOOD WORK IN ME
AND HE WILL KEEP WORKING IN ME.

MY HIDING PLACE

*You are my hiding place; You keep
me from trouble; You surround
me with songs of deliverance.*
PSALM 32:7 NASB

Lord Almighty, every so often I just need time to myself. I need time to think. I need time to get away from everyone else. When I do that, I feel like I can be completely alone with You. In the middle of this noisy world, I can quiet myself and be with You—my hiding place. Thank You that I can come to You when I'm worn out and need refreshing, when I'm scared and could use Your comfort, or when I'm in trouble and need help. You keep me safe, even when I don't realize it. When I feel like I'm in danger, I want to run to You. Please open my eyes to see You at work in my life. I know You're there every day, protecting me. Thank You! In Jesus' name I pray, amen.

GOD IS MY HIDING PLACE. I CAN RUN
TO HIM WHEN I'M IN TROUBLE.

LET YOUR LOVE SHOW

If you love each other, all men
will know you are My followers.
JOHN 13:35 NLV

Father, sometimes I wonder what You want me to do. How can I make You happy? How can I know I'm doing what You'd like me to do? But Your Word is so clear. Jesus explained exactly what His followers need to do: love! I am His follower, and I want to do what He asks. I want to love You and love others. I want to be known for my love! I pray You'll help my love grow for the people who are easy to love as well as for those who are pretty tough and seem unlovable. When I'm tempted to not act very lovingly, please fill me with Your love and let me pour it out to people around me. You could've asked me to do all kinds of things for You. Knowing that You've asked me to love is pretty amazing. Please help my love for other people start changing the world around me! In Jesus' name I pray, amen.

AS A FOLLOWER OF CHRIST,
I NEED TO LOVE OTHERS!

THAT HELPLESS FEELING

Arise, LORD! Lift up your hand,
O God. Do not forget the helpless.
PSALM 10:12 NIV

Lord, people haven't been treating me very kindly lately. Sometimes my so-called friends aren't very good friends. They've said or done things that have hurt my feelings. And mean kids have such a way of being nasty. I feel helpless! What people say about me or do to me is out of my control. Sometimes I wish I were invisible so I could not be treated badly. I need Your help! Please come to my defense. Please rise up and help me. Step into these difficult situations in some way and help me. And please comfort me and give me strength. I want to be a good example of Jesus and His love in these situations. In His name I pray, amen.

IT'S NORMAL TO FEEL HELPLESS.
WHEN I DO, I CAN TURN TO GOD FOR HELP.

A DIFFERENT FOCUS

*Set your minds on things that are above,
not on things that are on earth.*
COLOSSIANS 3:2 ESV

Father, it's so easy to get stuck on thinking about things of this world. I think about comfort and my stuff. I think about school, friends, activities, and things I want to do. I think about future plans and how I'd like things to be different than they are. So often I focus on me, me, me. But deep down, I want to set my mind on what really matters. It's not that my life doesn't matter, but I want to think about things that are eternal. Not the passing pleasures of life here, and not the small stuff. Belongings and experiences will come and go, but You last forever. My life is hidden in You through Christ, and when Christ appears again I'll get to share in His amazingness. When that happens, all of the little details of this world won't matter at all. How exciting! I can hardly wait for that day. Amen.

I DON'T HAVE TO OBSESS OVER THOUGHTS
OF THE LITTLE THINGS OF THE WORLD.
I NEED TO THINK ABOUT LASTING THINGS.

WAITING

*Wait for the Lord; Be strong and let your
heart take courage; Yes, wait for the Lord.*
PSALM 27:14 NASB

Lord, it's not so easy for me to wait. In fact, patience feels really, really hard. It's hard to wait for You, but I know I need to do it. I can't speed things up with all of my impatience. I can't rush things or force things to happen. Sometimes, I just need to wait on You and Your timing and plan. Please help me be brave and strong and courageous as I wait on You. Please help me trust You completely as I wait for You. And when my waiting is over, please help me realize the beautiful gifts You've so generously given. In Jesus' name I pray, amen.

I CAN BE STRONG AND COURAGEOUS
AS I WAIT FOR THE LORD.

REMEMBERING YOU

*Remember also your Maker while
you are young, before the days of
trouble come and the years when
you will say, "I have no joy in them."*
ECCLESIASTES 12:1 NLV

Father, You've made me in a wonderful way! I
want to think of You and remember that You're
part of my life every day. Right now, I'm young,
life is pretty good, and it seems like I have my
entire life before me. But I pray I won't take any
of this for granted. And I don't want to focus on
the pleasures of life right now and totally shut
You out or think I have time to worship You later
when I'm older. I want to praise You and follow
You now when times are good! I also want to
praise You and follow You later when times are
bad. Thank You so much for my friends and the
fun times in my life right now. Truly they're good
gifts from You. Let me remember that You're the
giver of all good things. I worship and thank
You! Amen.

NO MATTER HOW YOUNG OR OLD I AM,
I NEED TO REMEMBER AND FOLLOW THE LORD.

RADIANT

I sought the Lord and He answered me,
and rescued me from all my fears.
They looked to Him and were radiant,
and their faces will never be ashamed.

PSALM 34:4–5 NASB

Lord, when I seek You, I find You. When I call to You, You answer me! And when I honestly tell you what I'm afraid of, You relieve me from those fears. The more of myself that I bring to You—all my hopes, fears, dreams, failures—the more that I'll reflect Your radiance. The more that I get to know You, the more I'll shine. You'll replace my shame with honor. You'll replace my fear with courage. And You'll replace my weakness with strength. Apart from You, I'm like a wilted flower. My strength is sapped, my bloom is droopy. But You have the ability to make beauty spring out of me. You make me radiant. It's really quite amazing. Thank You!

WHEN I TURN TO THE LORD,
HE'LL REPLACE MY FEARS AND
WEAKNESS WITH COURAGE AND STRENGTH.

WHAT'S THAT TO ME?

Jesus answered, "If I want him to remain alive until I return, what is that to you? You must follow me."
JOHN 21:22 NIV

Father, so often I fixate on what other people are doing. I focus on what You're doing in and through their lives. It's easy for me to compare myself with others. But with You, every single person is unique. You have unique plans and purposes for every single person. Instead of comparing myself to others, help me remember to follow You and get busy working out the plans You have for me and my life. I can do what no one else can do. Please keep me focused on that work. Take my eyes off what You're doing with other people and help me get busy with what You've asked me to do. When I notice You opening doors in my life, I pray I'll take the opportunities. When I get to follow You in faith, I pray I will! Thank You for charting a completely different path for me than anyone else. In Jesus' name I pray, amen.

IF GOD CHOOSES TO USE PEOPLE IN
DIFFERENT WAYS, WHAT'S THAT
TO ME? I MUST FOLLOW HIM.

PURSUE PEACE

Turn away from evil and do good;
seek peace and pursue it.
PSALM 34:14 ESV

Father God, I love that You've called me to seek peace and pursue it. Peace won't happen on its own. In fact, peace seems like such a foreign concept in this world. People say they want peace, but with the hurtful and destructive things they say and do, all they bring is division and harm. But You've asked me to turn away from evil and do good. Please help me find ways to do good and to add peace to the situations You put me in. Instead of reacting in anger, please help me bring peace with the words I say and the things I do. When I disagree with someone, please help me not to think of myself better than I am. Instead, I pray You'll help me grow in quiet humility. Please help me be a peacemaker. In Jesus' name I pray, amen.

I NEED TO DO GOOD AND
CHASE AFTER PEACE!

MORE AND MORE

And this is my prayer: I pray that
your love will grow more and more.
I pray that you will have better
understanding and be wise in all things.
PHILIPPIANS 1:9 NLV

Lord, it's so special to think of my love growing more and more. I can imagine it growing a lot like a bud that starts out as a tiny, little shoot and grows into a tall, strong flowering plant. Just like a growing, thriving plant, I pray my love would grow super strong and healthy. I want my love to be productive, so that people around me would see and feel the effects of my love. As my love grows, I pray You'll bless me with wisdom and understanding, so I can discern what to do. A life of wisdom and love may seem like a pretty tall order, especially for a teenager. But I pray both would increase in my life every day. In Jesus' name I pray, amen.

THE LORD CAN HELP ME
GROW IN LOVE AND WISDOM.

A STEP OF FAITH

Give your way over to the Lord.
Trust in Him also. And He will do it.
PSALM 37:5 NLV

Lord, as much as I want to try to hold on to my life, including all my choices, I would be much better off if I fully trusted You and gave my way over to You. So here I am, ready to release my will to You. It's a big step of faith! But I give my way over to You. I surrender my hopes and my dreams. I trust that Your way for me is best. I feel like I'm taking a huge leap—almost like I'm stepping out into thin air and absolutely believing You won't let me stumble or fall. Please work in me and through me. As You do, I pray You'll reassure me with Your peace. I love You and I'm excited to see what You'll do in my life! In Jesus' name I pray, amen.

WHEN I TRUST THE LORD AND GIVE
MY WAY OVER TO HIM, HE WILL DO
AMAZING THINGS THROUGH ME!

I HAVE A CONFESSION TO MAKE. . .

If we confess our sins, he is faithful and just and will forgive us our sins and purify us from all unrighteousness.
1 JOHN 1:9 NIV

Father God, I have sinned. I've fallen short of Your perfection and have done wrong. I know I've done wrong. In fact, I was tempted and gave in to that temptation. But I'm sorry that I did. I feel guilty—and rightfully so! I am guilty. I want to confess my sin to You now. You know what I've done, but I need to confess it to You. I'm sorry I did this. I pray You'll forgive me and that I'll accept Your forgiveness. Please take away the guilt of my sin. Purify and cleanse me from what I've done wrong. I know You're faithful. I know You're able to forgive me, so I pray You will! I love You and want to live a life that's right in Your eyes. In Jesus' name I pray, amen.

WHEN I CONFESS MY SINS TO GOD,
HE WILL FORGIVE ME.

PRICELESS

How priceless is your unfailing love,
O God! People take refuge in the
shadow of your wings.
PSALM 36:7 NIV

Almighty God, Your love is better than anything this world has to offer. It's greater than any love any person could show me. It's so much more than I could ever give. You love me with so much kindness, favor, and mercy. Your love is priceless! It never fails, never gives up, and never ends. You're known by Your love, and Your followers are known by love. Love is Your trademark. I pray I'll experience it in a new way tonight. Any way You can help me feel loved by You, please do. I want to run to the shadow of Your wings for comfort and shelter. You are my safe place and my haven. Thank You! Amen.

GOD'S LOVE FOR ME NEVER FAILS.
HE COMFORTS ME WITH HIS PRICELESS LOVE.

CALL TO HIM

*"Call to Me and I will answer you,
and I will tell you great and mighty
things, which you do not know."*

JEREMIAH 33:3 NASB

Father, when I call to You, You'll answer me.
You'll even tell me things I don't know yet. I
pray I'll listen carefully for Your voice and watch
for how You'll gently lead me. Please help me
walk through doors You open for me. I pray I'll
bravely follow You, even when it feels like I'm
not comfortable or qualified. As I trust You to
work in me, I want to follow You in faith. When
things don't make sense to me, please give me
peace. I gladly admit I don't know everything. I
don't even know how I feel most days—or why
I feel the way I do. Please give me clarity. And
please give me good judgment, so I can live in
a way that brings You honor. In Jesus' name I
pray, amen.

WHEN I CALL TO GOD,
HE WILL ANSWER ME.

TRUSTING GOD AND DOING GOOD

Trust in the LORD and do good. Live in the land and cultivate faithfulness.

PSALM 37:3 NASB

Lord Almighty, You are worthy of my trust. I know You're reliable. I have total confidence in You. You make me feel safe. Thanks for giving me opportunities to trust You more. I admit that when I get to trust You, it's because I can't do something on my own. When things are out of my control, it feels scary and a little overwhelming. Instead of panicking or trying to figure things out on my own, I'd rather relax and trust You. As I'm waiting and trusting You, please help me do good. I don't want to react out of fear or frustration. I want to be faithful and good. Please help that goodness be a very real part of my life. In Jesus' name I pray, amen.

WHILE I'M TRUSTING GOD, I WANT
TO DO GOOD AND BE FAITHFUL.

LESS AND MORE

Nothing should be done because of pride or thinking about yourself. Think of other people as more important than yourself.
PHILIPPIANS 2:3 NLV

Father God, it is so incredibly easy to think about myself. And it's just as easy to try to make everything in this life about me. I want to think about how good or bad I am at certain things. I want to focus on what I'd like to have. It's fun to think about what things could make my future great. I'm so easily consumed by what makes me feel comfortable and what I prefer. But I need to get past myself. In fact, I need to stop thinking about myself so much. When I focus on me, me, me, I get filled with pride. I start loving myself more than other things and other people. As hard as it is to do, please help me think of other people as being more important than I am. Please help me start treating them like they're valued and loved. In Jesus' name I pray, amen.

I NEED TO STOP THINKING ABOUT MYSELF SO MUCH. I NEED TO START THINKING ABOUT OTHER PEOPLE MORE.

I'M GIFTED!

*There are different kinds of gifts. But it
is the same Holy Spirit Who gives them.
There are different kinds of work to be
done for Him. But the work is for the same
Lord. There are different ways of doing
His work. But it is the same God who
uses all these ways in all people.*
1 CORINTHIANS 12:4–6 NLV

Lord, thank You for giving me unique gifts and
talents. I pray I'll use them boldly and creatively
for You! Please help me become more of a creator
instead of only consuming what other people
create. I'd love to become a creator so I can
impact this world for You in the special way
You've blessed me. Please help me influence
people around me as I do the different kinds of
work for You. Also, please help me develop and
nurture the gifts You've given me instead of being
afraid or too shy to use them. I want to shine for
You! And I want to use what You've given me in
a special way. In Jesus' name I pray, amen.

**THE LORD HAS GIVEN ME UNIQUE
GIFTS I CAN USE TO WORK FOR HIM.**

LOVE IS A VERB

*Dear children, let us not love with words
or speech but with actions and in truth.*
1 JOHN 3:18 NIV

Lord, so often I get a wrong picture of love. I think of love in a romantic sense, like marriage. Or I think of love in a cutesy, Valentine-y sort of way, like puppies, kitties, and flowers. I can even think of love in terms of my favorite things—like how much I love ice cream or sleeping in. But true love isn't about that. Real, actual love is more than just saying "I love you." It's so important for me to actually love through the things I do. I need to act on my love. I need to do the hard things and make my love an action—just like a verb. The thoughts or feelings of love aren't enough. I actually need to do something about my love. So I pray I will! I pray I'll be known for showing my love for You with everyone I meet. In Jesus' name I pray, amen.

I CAN'T JUST TALK ABOUT MY LOVE.
I NEED TO SHOW MY LOVE IN MY ACTIONS.

HOW CAN I BE RIGHTEOUS?

*When the righteous cry for help,
the LORD hears and delivers them
out of all their troubles.*

PSALM 34:17 ESV

Lord, when I think of being righteous, I think of someone who is right, or without sin. Jesus was the only perfect, sinless person. Because I sin every day, I'm far from righteous. Even if I try to do good, it falls far from Your perfection. But through Jesus, I've been made right with You. And through the way Your Holy Spirit works in my heart You can do beautiful things in me. I'll never be righteous on my own. But You have the power to work through me, and You can produce righteousness in my life that only comes from You. I want to follow You. I want You to work in my heart and in my life. As I chase after You, I can be sure that You hear my cries for help and that You'll deliver me from my troubles. Thank You for listening and answering! Amen.

I CAN BE RIGHT WITH GOD THROUGH JESUS.
WHEN I AM MADE RIGHT, HE'LL HEAR
AND ANSWER MY PRAYERS.

WHATEVER!

And whatever you do, in word or deed,
do everything in the name of the Lord Jesus,
giving thanks to God the Father through him.
COLOSSIANS 3:17 ESV

Father God, it's pretty neat to realize that the things I say and do can be done for You. There's purpose in what I say! The things I do matter! And for as much as I'm tempted to think that I don't matter, that's completely untrue. Whatever I say can be said to give You thanks and to bring Christ glory. And whatever I do is proof that Christ is Lord of my life. My words, actions, and choices all show where my heart is. I want to remember this! When I'm tempted to say or do selfish—or even cruel!—things, please help me remember that I'm saying words and doing deeds for You. Not myself. And not to benefit anyone else, but for You. Thank You that I can say and do all things for Jesus. In His name I pray, amen.

WHATEVER I SAY OR DO SHOULD
BE DONE IN THE NAME OF JESUS.

STOP STRESSING

Be still, and know that I am God.
I will be exalted among the nations,
I will be exalted in the earth!
PSALM 46:10 ESV

Father, You are God. You have created absolutely everything, including this earth. It's easy for me to focus on what I see every day. I see chaos in the world and problems around me. Relationships both thrill and frustrate me. I find myself thinking so much about what has happened or what could happen. And as I get lost in these thoughts, I lose my focus on who You are. But I can stop stressing and striving. I can just be quiet and know You are God. You're in control. You have a purpose and a plan that can't be ruined. You'll be lifted up or exalted on earth. All people will know You alone are God. I don't have to worry about what might happen. And I don't have to fear the future. You are God. I can be still as I worship and trust You completely. In Your holy name I pray, amen.

BECAUSE GOD IS GOD, I CAN
STOP STRESSING AND STRIVING.

A SEEKER

Seek the LORD, all you humble of the land,
you who do what he commands.
Seek righteousness, seek humility.
ZEPHANIAH 2:3 NIV

O Lord, You've asked me to search diligently to find You. And You've asked me to search for righteousness and humility. When I seek You and see You for who You are—You are the Creator God! The perfect One who knows all and can do all!—I'm easily humbled. Any chance that I'll be puffed up with my own pride and self-dependence is quickly deflated when I consider who You are. You are the necessity of my life, so I'll gladly try to do what You command. Sometimes, as much as I try, I stumble. Could You please help me? I'm willing to do what You ask. It's just difficult for me to attempt to live right on my own. That's why I need Jesus so much. Please help me! I trust that You can equip me to do Your work. And I trust that as I look to You, You'll show mercy and help me. Amen.

I NEED TO SEEK THE LORD! AND I NEED
TO TRY TO LIVE A HUMBLE, RIGHT LIFE.

WAITING

*I waited patiently for the L*ORD*;*
he inclined to me and heard my cry.
PSALM 40:1 ESV

Lord, patience doesn't seem to come easily to me! In fact, it's really hard for me to wait. And it's really hard to be patient. But You're trustworthy and true. I can wait for You. And as I pray to You, You hear my prayers. You hear my cries for help and listen to what's on my heart. Thank You! I pray my patience will grow and grow. Help me wait for You without complaining. When I wonder if or when You'll answer me, I pray I'll remember who You are instead of focusing on my own desires. Even if it feels new or even a little strange at first, I'd love for my life to be more about You and less about me. In Your name I pray, amen.

THE LORD HEARS ME. I CAN
WAIT PATIENTLY FOR HIM.

TWO COMMANDS

*This is His commandment, that we believe
in the name of His Son Jesus Christ, and love
one another, just as He commanded us.*
1 JOHN 3:23 NASB

Father God, Jesus taught that there are two commands that should rule my life: I need to love You and love others like I love myself. Jesus' disciple John taught that I need to believe in the name of Jesus Christ and love others. I can love You. I can believe in Jesus. And as hard as it sometimes feels, I can love others too. People aren't always lovable. And people don't always act in ways that make me want to love them. But I need to anyway. Love needs to be what I'm known for. Love needs to be at the center of everything I do. It's definitely not easy. But I pray You'll help me love anyway, even when I don't feel like it. I pray that my belief in Christ would show through my love for others. In Jesus' name I pray, amen.

I NEED TO BELIEVE IN JESUS CHRIST
AND LOVE OTHER PEOPLE.

WHEN TROUBLE HITS

*Why are you sad, O my soul? Why have
you become troubled within me? Hope in
God, for I will praise Him again for
His help of being near me.*
PSALM 42:5 NLV

Father, my thoughts are consumed by the troubles in my life. Deep down I feel sad, and I think it's because so much is out of my control. Things seem bad. Nothing seems to work out. I don't know how to right the wrongs or if they can even be made right. So much seems to be off, and definitely not in a good way. I pray I'll keep trusting in You. My hope can rest in You. You can make things right. Please give me strength to get through these trials. You can make a way when it seems there is no way. You're always near me. You know what's going on, even when I don't. Please help me! Please increase my trust as I'm in this tough situation. I love You and want to trust You. Please faithfully guide me and provide for my needs. In Jesus' name I pray, amen.

EVEN WHEN I FACE TROUBLES,
I CAN HOPE IN GOD.

THE EYES OF MY HEART

I pray that the eyes of your heart may be enlightened in order that you may know the hope to which he has called you, the riches of his glorious inheritance in his holy people.

EPHESIANS 1:18 NIV

Father, my heart—my soul—is the center of all my thoughts, desires, appetites, and affections. It's me! It's what I believe and what I cherish most. Could you please enlighten the eyes of my heart? Help me clearly see and know the hope You've given me. You've actually called me to Your hope that one day will be reality. And You've promised that I'm Your heir. Someday I'll actually receive Your riches. Thank You! These promises are so amazing. When I think of You and all You offer me, I pray I'll let my hope and trust in You change my thinking. I don't want to focus on what's going on right now and will eventually pass away. Even when it feels tough, I want my heart to focus on You and what will last forever. In Jesus' name I pray, amen.

I WANT THE EYES OF MY HEART TO SEE WHAT LASTS—THE LORD'S PROMISES.

MY SAFE PLACE, STRENGTH, AND HELP

God is our safe place and our strength.
He is always our help when we are in trouble.
PSALM 46:1 NLV

Lord God, thank You for being my safe place!
And thank You for being my strength. Sometimes I definitely feel in danger—or I feel like
everything I know is crumbling right before
my eyes. And sometimes I feel absolutely weak.
I know in my heart of hearts that I can't go on
in my own strength. But You are strong! And
You are safe. When I know I'm in trouble, You'll
help me. Your help might come in ways that are
totally surprising, but it comes. And Your safety,
strength, and help might come in surprising ways
or predictable ones. But the amazing fact is that
You do come through for me. I can fully trust
You to work in a wonderful way. Thank You! In
Your holy name I pray, amen.

GOD IS MY SAFE PLACE,
MY STRENGTH, AND MY HELP.

WHO IS JESUS?

If anyone acknowledges that Jesus is the Son of God, God lives in them and they in God.
1 JOHN 4:15 NIV

Father, I believe that Jesus is Your son. I believe He came to earth in a pretty miraculous way. And I believe He lived a perfect, sinless life, then was killed. After He died, He came back to life—He resurrected—and lives today. Your Word describes this in detail, and I believe it! When I have questions or doubts, I pray I'll study what Your Word says. Please answer my questions. Please relieve my doubts. Because I do believe Jesus defeated death, I don't have to fear. That's so incredibly freeing! Since I believe in Jesus, You live in me through Your Holy Spirit. I'm not alone because You're always with me. This truly is such a wonderful thing. Thank You, Lord!

WHEN I BELIEVE AND SAY JESUS IS
THE SON OF GOD, GOD LIVES IN ME.

WHAT A BAD DAY!

O Lord, hear my prayer, and listen to
my cry. Do not be quiet when You see
my tears. For I am a stranger with You,
a visitor like all my fathers.

PSALM 39:12 NLV

Lord, I cry out to You! I had such a rough day.
I can't believe what's happened to me. I am so
upset. In fact, in all the crumminess of today, I
feel really distant from You. I pray You'll listen
to me and hear my prayers. As I cry, I pray You'll
see my tears. Could You please comfort me?
Could You let me know in some way that You
see me, You hear me, and You know all that I'm
going through? I want to trust You especially in
the most difficult parts of my life. Please redeem
this awful day. Please make goodness come out
of all of the bad I'm facing. I love You and I'm
thankful I can cry out to You. In Jesus' name I
pray, amen.

ON BAD DAYS, I CAN CRY OUT
TO MY HEAVENLY FATHER.

SHOUTS OF JOY

The Lord your God is with you,
a Powerful One Who wins the battle.
He will have much joy over you.
With His love He will give you new life.
He will have joy over you with loud singing.
ZEPHANIAH 3:17 NLV

Lord God, You are with me! And You actually take a lot of joy in me. Sometimes it seems really hard to believe that I could bring You joy. Especially because I know You are mighty. You're so powerful, You can and do win any battle. Even though You are the Mighty One, I still bring You joy. Thank You for Your love, because with it, You give me new life. Through Your love that comes from Jesus, I'm not the old me anymore. I'm a new creation. Not only do You fill me with Your love, but You also shower me with Your joy. Shouts of joy! Joy that can't be contained. You give me so many amazing things, like life, love, and joy. Thank You! I want to praise You and thank You for Your goodness forever! Amen.

THE LORD MY GOD IS
WITH ME! HE LOVES ME!

SOME HEART WORK

Create in me a clean heart, O God,
and renew a right spirit within me.
PSALM 51:10 ESV

My Lord and God, I feel like I need a do-over. I could use a fresh start. I'm tired of my sins. I'm sorry for my attitude and the way I've behaved lately. I know I should change. And I want to change. I just don't know how to do it on my own. In reality, I can't change on my own. All of my attempts will only be attempts. You're the One who can change me. You can create a clean heart in me. Please do! And You're the One to renew my spirit so it's firmly established and fixed on You. Please repair my spirit so it's securely set on You. You're the One who can make all things new. I pray You would do this in my life! In Jesus' name I pray, amen.

GOD CAN TRANSFORM MY
HEART AND REPAIR MY SPIRIT.

WHERE IS THE GOOD WAY?

This is what the Lord says: "Stand at the
crossroads and look; ask for the ancient
paths, ask where the good way is, and walk
in it, and you will find rest for your souls."
JEREMIAH 6:16 NIV

Lord of heaven and earth, You are good. You've
created good things I can enjoy, and You've explained a good way to live. Your good way will
help me live closely with You, and it won't be a
burden. In fact, Your good way gives me rest for
my weary soul. Thank You! It's so kind of You
to offer me goodness. I pray I'll seek after Your
goodness and take it. Please guard my heart
from the affections and desires of this world.
Please show me where Your good way is! I want
to follow it and walk in it. I long for Your rest.
I'm ready to stop striving for myself and trying
to live in my own power. I surrender my life to
You and pray You'll refresh me with Your very
good way. In Your name I pray, amen.

GOD WILL GIVE ME A GOOD WAY.
WHEN I WALK IN IT, I'LL FIND REST.

AM I LOOKING?

God has looked down from heaven at the children of men to see if there is anyone who understands and looks for God.

PSALM 53:2 NLV

Father God, I know You see me! I know You know me! And I know Your ways are higher than my ways. I don't understand everything You do, but I pray You'll fill me with Your wisdom so I can make wise choices in my life. I'll admit that many days I go right ahead with my own plans and purposes. I try to figure things out on my own and just kind of drift along. But, Lord, I want to look for You in the details of my days! I'd like Your guidance, please. Just as You look at me, I want to look for You! When You look at me, I want You to see I'm living for You. And as I face decisions or challenges in my days, I pray I'll ask You for help. Please make it obvious You're listening and answering my prayers in amazing ways. I love You!

GOD KNOWS WHEN I'M LOOKING
FOR HIM AND WHEN I'M NOT.

I AM FREE

*Live as people who are free, not using
your freedom as a cover-up for evil,
but living as servants of God.*
1 PETER 2:16 ESV

Father God, through Christ You've given me freedom. I pray I'll live like I'm free, and not like I'm in bondage. I don't have to live like I'm enslaved to the things of this world. I don't have to be a slave to the thoughts or belongings or my status or anything else. You love me. You've forgiven me. And You've placed me exactly where I am at exactly this moment in time for a reason. I pray I'll live for You as Your servant. I'd love to do the work You have planned for me. I don't want to take advantage of my freedom just to sin or live like I'm part of this world. Please help me remember that I'm set apart for You. And I'm free. In Jesus' powerful name I pray, amen.

I DON'T HAVE TO LIVE LIKE
I'M A SLAVE TO THE WORLD.
CHRIST HAS GIVEN ME FREEDOM!

SAYING AND BELIEVING

If you confess with your mouth that Jesus is Lord and believe in your heart that God raised him from the dead, you will be saved. For with the heart one believes and is justified, and with the mouth one confesses and is saved.

ROMANS 10:9–10 ESV

Father, thank You that Your Word so clearly tells me what I need to do to be saved. All I need to do is say—out loud—that Jesus is Lord. And what I need to truly believe deep down is that You've raised Jesus from the dead. That belief will make me right with You. When I actually say that Jesus is Lord, You save me from the punishment of my sin. Your salvation—the way You save me—is utterly amazing and nothing I could ever do on my own. Father, I do believe Jesus is Lord and You've raised Him from the dead! I praise You for that. In Jesus' name I pray, amen.

TO BE SAVED FROM THE PUNISHMENT OF MY SINS, I NEED TO CONFESS WITH MY MOUTH THAT JESUS IS LORD, AND I NEED TO BELIEVE IN MY HEART THAT GOD RAISED HIM FROM THE DEAD.

LOOK OUT!

Do not merely look out for your own personal interests, but also for the interests of others.
PHILIPPIANS 2:4 NASB

Father God, as hard as it is for me to say, I admit that I'm selfish. I admit I look out for myself a lot. I like what I like, and I focus a lot of my thoughts and energies on what I like. Instead of only looking out for things that interest me, I pray I'll start thinking about other people too. Please help me be an encouraging cheerleader to other people. Help me think about what other people might want or need. Instead of focusing only on myself, please help me think of ways to focus on other people. When I do, I pray You'll refresh me and help me to see the joy that comes from loving others the same way I love myself. Your unselfish way of thinking of others is a really good thing—please help me realize and remember how good it is. In Jesus' name I pray, amen.

I NEED TO STOP LOOKING OUT FOR MYSELF
SO MUCH AND START LOOKING OUT
FOR OTHER PEOPLE TOO.

GIVING MY WORRIES

Give all your cares to the Lord and He will give you strength. He will never let those who are right with Him be shaken.

PSALM 55:22 NLV

Lord, I'm feeling weighed down by my concerns and worries. I think about what's happening in my life right now, and I wonder what might happen in the future. It's really easy to focus on the negative. I don't want to throw a big pity party for myself, though, because that only leaves me feeling more depressed. And I don't want to stress out about what might or might not happen. I can't live my life worrying about what might happen someday or what could go wrong. Father, I give You my cares tonight. I'm handing over all of my burdens with what's really happening and all of my worries of what might happen. I surrender all of my stress to You! I don't know what will happen, but I know You're in control. And You are powerful. I pray that You'll fill me with Your strength and peace. Amen.

WHEN I SURRENDER ALL MY WORRIES,
CONCERNS, AND STRESS TO THE LORD,
HE WILL GIVE ME STRENGTH.

JUSTICE, MERCY, AND COMPASSION

This is what the Lord Almighty said: "Administer true justice; show mercy and compassion to one another. Do not oppress the widow or the fatherless, the foreigner or the poor. Do not plot evil against each other."
ZECHARIAH 7:9–10 NIV

Lord Almighty, You care very deeply about how people are treated. You never turn a blind eye to injustice. The qualities of Your character show me what You value: mercy, compassion, justice, helpfulness, and goodness. I pray I'll live a just life and be fair to every single person. You've shown me so much mercy, so I want to show mercy to everyone I meet, even if it feels difficult. And I want to sincerely be concerned about other people. Please show me ways to help any widows or orphans I know, along with poor people and new people to my school and community. I pray You'll help me think of ways to bless others, and I pray for the courage to follow through and actually do those good things. In Jesus' name I pray, amen.

THE LORD WANTS ME TO TREAT OTHER PEOPLE WITH JUSTICE, MERCY, AND COMPASSION, AND TO HELP THE HELPLESS.

TEARS IN A BOTTLE

You have taken account of my
miseries; Put my tears in Your
bottle. Are they not in Your book?
PSALM 56:8 NASB

Father, You know all things. You know what
I've been thinking and feeling. You know my
confusion and doubts. You know when I'm disappointed and feel brokenhearted. You know
when I'm angry and hurt. The way I feel matters
to You. In fact, You care so much for me You
could put my tears in a bottle. As You know and
understand what I'm going through and how I'm
feeling, comfort me in a very real way. Please
calm my heart and help me snuggle into Your
kind, caring protection. I pray I'll find peace in
You. Please refresh me and restore my hope in
You. In Jesus' name I pray, amen.

THE LORD KNOWS EXACTLY WHAT I'M GOING
THROUGH AND HOW I'M FEELING. HE PAYS
ATTENTION TO EVERYTHING I'M EXPERIENCING.

LIFE

And this is the testimony: God has given
us eternal life, and this life is in his Son.
Whoever has the Son has life; whoever does
not have the Son of God does not have life.
1 JOHN 5:11–12 NIV

Father God, thank You for Jesus! Thank You for sending Him—Your Son—to this world so that any person who believes in Him would have eternal life. That's life forever! Life with You that won't go away! That forever kind of life is found only in Jesus, not in the things that I do or anything that I earn. At some point in my life, I need to make the decision if I have the Son. If I haven't decided yet, then I don't have life. Father, I want to take the time right now to choose. I believe in Jesus! Today I'm making the decision that I believe in Jesus Christ. Thank You for Your amazing gift of forever life that comes only through Him. In His name I pray, amen.

GOD HAS GIVEN FOREVER
LIFE IN JESUS CHRIST.

A PURPOSE FOR ME

I cry out to God Most High, to God
who fulfills his purpose for me.
PSALM 57:2 ESV

God Most High, You have a purpose for me. That's so amazing! You care about me and value my life so much that You have planned what You'd like me to do. And then You've gone ahead to fulfill that purpose for me. You make it happen! Even if I don't understand everything or see all the details right now, You're at work even now. When I get older, I'll be able to look back at this part of my life and see how You're using it for good. What I face today or tomorrow will shape me. I pray You'll choose to use me for Your good work. And when I'm discouraged and losing hope, please listen as I cry out to You. I want to trust You completely as You're working out Your plan for me day by day. I love You! Amen.

GOD HAS A UNIQUE PURPOSE FOR ME!
HE WILL WORK TO FULFILL THAT
PURPOSE IN MY LIFE.

REJOICE!

Rejoice in the Lord always.
I will say it again: Rejoice!
PHILIPPIANS 4:4 NIV

Lord God, thank You for filling me with joy! Even when my circumstances and situations in life don't seem ideal—or when things seem downright crummy—I'm glad I can still rejoice in You. My joy in You will give me strength. I pray You'll fill me with Your Holy Spirit and help me walk by Your Spirit so Your joy can pour out of me. I want to trust You more and more. As I do, please help me rejoice in You in good times and in bad times. You are faithful and kind. You are worthy of my trust and my praise. Thank You for loving me and giving me a reason to rejoice! In Your holy name I pray, amen.

I CAN ALWAYS REJOICE IN
THE LORD. HE FILLS ME WITH JOY.

I'M HEARD

*But God has surely listened
and has heard my prayer.*
PSALM 66:19 NIV

Father God, when I pray to You, You listen to me. That's pretty amazing! When I consider that the Lord of the universe, the Maker of heaven and earth, the beginning and the end, listens to me, it's pretty mind-boggling. I definitely don't feel like I deserve Your attention. Sometimes it feels like my own family and friends don't pay attention to me as much as I'd like, and even if they do pay attention, they don't always understand me. But You always pay attention to me. And You understand me completely. What I say and think and feel truly matters to You. You listen and hear my prayers. Thank You! Your concern and care and attention show me how very much You love me. I pray I'll start listening to You and hearing You more. In Jesus' name I pray, amen.

GOD LISTENS TO ME!
HE HEARS MY PRAYERS!

GOOD!

Dear friend, do not imitate what is evil but what is good. Anyone who does what is good is from God. Anyone who does what is evil has not seen God.

3 JOHN 11 NIV

Father, I've heard that imitation is the sincerest form of flattery. But so often, it's hard to find things that truly are worth imitating. I pray I'll start imitating the good things I see in this world. When people do good, I want to imitate it. And when I notice evil attitudes and words and deeds, I pray I'll flee. I don't want to dwell on evil thoughts, and I don't want to imitate evil things. Please help me discern and wisely judge what is good and what is not. Please fill me with Your Spirit so that goodness is a part of my thoughts, words, and actions. I love You and want to spend my life doing Your good works in the world around me! In Your name I pray, amen.

DOING GOOD THINGS COMES
OUT OF MY LOVE FOR GOD.

NEEDING STRENGTH

Hear my cry, O God; listen to my prayer.
From the ends of the earth I call to you, I call
as my heart grows faint; lead me to the rock
that is higher than I. For you have been my
refuge, a strong tower against the foe.
PSALM 61:1–3 NIV

My Lord and my God, I need You. I'm down and worn out and heartbroken. My heart feels so out of sorts I feel like giving up. Thank You for listening to me and loving me right now. I don't have to get my act together. I don't have to pretend I'm someone I'm not to make You think of me differently. I love that I can come just as I am and You love me. You listen to me. You're my safe place. You're the strong tower I can run to when I feel like I'm attacked. I'm so thankful You're my strong rock and safe place of protection. Because of You, Your strength, might, and love, I don't have to fear. In Your holy name I pray, amen.

GOD IS MY STRONG PLACE OF PROTECTION,
EVEN WHEN I FEEL BEAT UP BY THE WORLD.

BEAUTIFUL

He has made everything
beautiful in its time.
ECCLESIASTES 3:11 ESV

Lord, the promise that You have made everything beautiful in its time is so comforting. Right now, I feel like I'm in the middle of a whole bunch of ugly. Nothing seems to be working out right. My hopes seem futile and my plans seem ruined. Please help me step back and see that You have a bigger and better picture. You have a plan and even if things are uncomfortable and disappointing now, You can and will make it all beautiful. You will bring beauty from these ashes in my life. When I feel like I'm in a hopeless situation, please help me trust that I can find hope in You. Please open my eyes to see glimmers of the beautiful work You're doing. I can't wait to see how You'll work in my life. Please help me patiently wait for You and keep loving You and honoring You with my words and attitudes, even as I wait. In Your precious name I pray, amen.

IN TIME, GOD WILL MAKE
ALL THINGS BEAUTIFUL.

NEVER LET ME GO

Even when you are old I will be the same.
And even when your hair turns white, I will
help you. I will take care of what I have made.
I will carry you, and will save you.
ISAIAH 46:4 NLV

Father, You're the one constant in my life. People come and go—some by choice, some by chance. Even the people who love me most might be taken from me through tragedy. But You'll never let me go. You will always be there for me. Even if I live to be an old lady, You will be the same. Even if I get all wrinkly and my white hair starts falling out and it hurts to move, You'll be with me, helping me every single day. You promise to take care of what You've made, and You've made me. You will carry me through my darkest, roughest days and nights. You save me from circumstances in my life, and You save me from an eternity separated from You. Thank You! It's a huge comfort to know You are always there for me. Amen.

THROUGHOUT MY LIFE, GOD ALWAYS
WILL BE THE SAME. HE ALWAYS
WILL HELP AND CARE FOR ME.

RESCUED!

*I am not ashamed of the Good News. It is
the power of God. It is the way He saves
men from the punishment of their sins if
they put their trust in Him. It is for the
Jew first and for all other people also.*
ROMANS 1:16 NLV

Lord, I am so thankful for Your Word! I'm thankful for the Good News of Jesus that runs through all the pages of scripture. That Good News—the gospel—is powerful! It tells me all about the way You planned my rescue. Through Jesus, You've saved me from the punishment of all I've done wrong. Both my intentional and unintentional sins are forgiven when I put my trust in Christ. Thank You for sending a rescuer! I'm glad for what He's done for me and in my life. Please help me boldly tell others about Him! I want to share Your Good News without fear and without shame. I'd love to help others by telling them how they can be rescued by Jesus too. I pray this all in the saving name of Jesus, amen.

GOD'S GOOD NEWS TELLS HOW
JESUS WAS SENT TO RESCUE ME
FROM THE PUNISHMENT OF MY SINS.

SEEK AND FIND

God, You are my God; I shall be watching for You; My soul thirsts for You, my flesh yearns for You, in a dry and exhausted land where there is no water.

PSALM 63:1 NASB

O God, You are my God. When I'm distracted by life and friends and school and stress, I long for You. When I focus on the details of my days and get consumed by what's happening in my life and in the world, I feel so parched. My soul is thirsty. I would love to be refreshed by You. I pray I'll come to You instead of trying to quench my thirst with pleasures of the world. You're my living water! You're the only One who will satisfy what I truly need. Because You're the One who satisfies, I want to seek You. You've promised that when I seek You, I'll find You. As I fall asleep tonight, please fill me with Your Spirit. When I wake up tomorrow, please help me remember to not get so caught up in the little things of this life. Amen.

I SHOULD SEEK GOD BECAUSE HE'S THE ONLY ONE WHO CAN QUENCH WHAT MY SOUL THIRSTS.

UNIFIED

*Finally, all of you, have unity of mind,
sympathy, brotherly love, a tender
heart, and a humble mind.*
1 PETER 3:8 ESV

Father, so often it's easy to think of myself. I like to do things my own way, and think my opinion is right and the best. When other people oppose me or simply have different opinions, I don't like it. And I don't accept the differences very well. But Your Word tells me to have unity of mind with other believers. That means if someone else believes in Christ, I need to try to live united instead of divided. And I need to live with love and sympathy for others. I need to step out of my own bubble and carefully respect what others have to say. Please help me love with a tender heart. And please help me stop thinking so highly of myself. I want to obey You, and I know You want Your followers to be known by their love for each other. In Your name I pray, amen.

I'M NOT THE CENTER OF THE UNIVERSE.
I NEED TO HUMBLY LOVE OTHER BELIEVERS
AND TRY TO BE UNIFIED INSTEAD OF DIVIDED.

I WANT TO PRAISE YOU!

My lips will praise You because Your loving-kindness is better than life.
PSALM 63:3 NLV

Father, You are so very good to me! I'm absolutely blown away by the good things You've done in my life. You definitely make my life better. And You care for every single one of my needs. I don't have to worry about a thing because You provide for me. Even before I realize I need something, You're already working on providing it in ways I'd never imagine. Thank You! Your loving-kindness really is better than life. I praise You for Your faithful love. I thank You for the amazing ways You care for me. I praise You for being a good, good God. I pray that I won't take anything You do for granted. And I pray that I'll remember it's You doing the work and providing for me and my needs—it's not me or the way I try to orchestrate things. Thank You for all that You do for me. I love You!

WHEN I SEE THE WAYS GOD LOVES AND CARES FOR ME, I CAN AND SHOULD PRAISE HIM!

EVERYBODY KNOWS

Men know about God. He has made it plain to them. Men cannot say they do not know about God. From the beginning of the world, men could see what God is like through the things He has made. This shows His power that lasts forever. It shows that He is God.
ROMANS 1:19–20 NLV

Father, You've made it abundantly clear who You are. There's no mystery or doubt that there's a supreme God over all creation. You show Your power in all sorts of things that happen in the world. If I look in the sky, I see how amazing the sun, moon, stars, and clouds are. If I look at the ground, I can inspect a blade of grass or a grain of sand and see Your creative power at work. Or if I examine my own hand and think about everything that works together so perfectly, it's obvious You've knit my body together with an amazing plan. Thank You for making Your existence so obvious! I worship You as Lord of all. Amen.

GOD HAS MADE IT BLATANTLY OBVIOUS THAT HE IS GOD. I CHOOSE TO BELIEVE HIM AND RECOGNIZE HIS WORK ALL AROUND ME.

A REASON TO COMPLAIN

O God, hear my voice when I complain.
Keep my life safe from the fear
of those who hate me.
PSALM 64:1 NLV

Lord, I haven't had a very good day. In fact, today I feel a little whiny. It seems like I have so much to complain about. For starters, I don't feel like I've been treated very fairly. Whether it was what someone else said about me or did to me, it wasn't very loving at all. In fact, it hurt my feelings. I'm tempted to dwell on that hurt and keep bringing it up in my heart and mind. I don't like it when people mistreat me. I pray You'll help me love others well even when I have a reason to complain and even when I'm tempted to fear my enemies. I'd rather live my life trusting You instead of fearing mean people. When people are mean to me, I want to remember that I can be completely honest and complain to You. Thanks for listening! Thanks for caring! In Jesus' name I pray, amen.

WHEN PEOPLE ARE MEAN TO ME,
I CAN COMPLAIN TO GOD.

STRONG TO SAVE

My soul is quiet and waits for God alone.
He is the One Who saves me. He alone is my
rock and the One Who saves me. He is my
strong place. I will not be shaken.
PSALM 62:1–2 NLV

Father God, I wait for You. I know You alone can save me. I definitely can't save myself! Because I know that You are my rock and my strength, I pray I'll depend completely on You. Please help me quiet my soul as I look to You for my strength and salvation. I want to put aside everything else that competes for my attention and affection. I don't want to trust in things of this world—not possessions, not power, not popularity, not my position or influence with my friends and family. And I don't want to trust in myself or my own power or strength. No, I lay all of this at Your feet as a sacrifice. I want to trust You and You alone. You are more than strong enough to save me. I love You! In Jesus' name I pray, amen.

GOD IS MY STRONG PLACE. HE SAVES ME!

YOUR FAVOR

I begged for Your favor with all my heart.
Show me Your love because of Your Word.
PSALM 119:58 NLV

Father, Your favor is what I truly want. When You show me Your favor, amazing things happen. But please help me be careful to not treat You and Your favor like a genie in a bottle. As much as I'd like to see Your favor in my life, I don't want to base my devotion to You on what You will or won't do for me. I want to stay faithful to You no matter what. Even when times are tough and it seems like You're just not there, or all sorts of awful things are happening around me, I still want to faithfully love and serve You. No matter how You choose to answer my prayers, I pray I'll keep my eyes and affection on You. As I do, I pray You'll also show Your love for me. Thanks in advance for the way You so lovingly care and provide for me, Father. In Your name I pray, amen.

I CAN ASK THE LORD FOR
HIS FAVOR IN MY LIFE.

WHATEVER I DO

Whatever work you do, do it with all your heart. Do it for the Lord and not for men. Remember that you will get your reward from the Lord. He will give you what you should receive. You are working for the Lord Christ.
COLOSSIANS 3:23–24 NLV

Lord God, as hard as it is for me to remember, this life is not about me. And the things I do aren't for my own benefit. I get caught up in thinking about and working for myself and my own good. I wonder and worry about what other people think of me and what I do. Could You please change my thinking? Whatever I do, please help me do it for You—not halfheartedly, but with all of me. As I work for You, please remind me that You're the One who will give me just what I should receive. When I get tired, renew my strength and energy so I can work with all of my heart just for You. In Jesus' name I pray, amen.

I'M WORKING FOR THE LORD CHRIST.
BECAUSE OF THAT, I NEED TO WORK
WITH ALL OF MY HEART.

PLEASE ANSWER ME

But as for me, my prayer is to You, Lord, at an acceptable time; God, in the greatness of Your mercy, answer me with Your saving truth.

PSALM 69:13 NASB

O Lord, I love You. You are so kind and loving. You listen to my prayers and know all that I face. I pray You'd answer me. Please! I know I can trust You. I know I can tell You all the little details that are on my mind tonight, and I'm so grateful for that. Out of the greatness of Your love for me, please answer my prayers. As I wait for You, please help my patience grow. When I'm tempted to feel frustrated, please fill me with Your peace. I know You are true and that You'll answer me in truth at just the right time. In Jesus' name I pray, amen.

WHEN I PRAY TO GOD,
HE WILL ANSWER ME.

MADE RIGHT

*Now that we have been made right
with God by putting our trust in Him,
we have peace with Him. It is because
of what our Lord Jesus Christ did for us.*

ROMANS 5:1 NLV

Father God, thank You for Jesus! Thank You for
His sacrifice for me. He loved me so much that
He was willing to die so His perfection would
replace my imperfection. That reality is humbling because I definitely don't deserve a gift like
that. Whether I deserve it or not, He made that
sacrifice. I put my trust in Him completely! As I
do, I know that I've been made right with You, all
because of Jesus. I'm so glad I have peace with
You, and forgiveness and acceptance through
Christ alone. Thank You for this enormous gift! I
am so relieved I'm made right with You. In Jesus'
holy name I pray, amen.

I AM MADE RIGHT WITH GOD
WHEN I PUT MY TRUST IN JESUS.

WATCHING AND WAITING

But as for me, I watch in hope
for the LORD, I wait for God
my Savior; my God will hear me.
MICAH 7:7 NIV

Lord, when I think about my life, I spend a lot of time waiting. I wait for the school year to pass so summer vacation can get here. I wait to get older so I'm allowed to do more things. A lot of weeks I wait for Friday so I can have some time for myself on the weekend. One person I wait for is You. I wait for You to work out Your plan in this world and in my life. I watch for You in hope that You'll move and do a good work in my life and in my heart. I pray that I won't get tired of waiting for You. Please help me make the most of the time I spend waiting. Instead of just keeping a countdown until my next big thing, I pray I'll do Your work in the world around me. I'm putting all of my hope and trust in You, Lord! In Your name I pray, amen.

I CAN WATCH IN HOPE AND
WAIT FOR GOD, MY SAVIOR.

GOD IS MY HELP

*Surely God is my help; the Lord
is the one who sustains me.*
PSALM 54:4 NIV

Father God, You strengthen and support me. When I need help—and oh, I do!—You are there for me. I don't have to fear. Please help me when I can't understand something in a lesson at school. And when I'm having trouble with relationships—either with bullies or friends who have hurt my feelings or family members who seem to be especially grouchy—please help me trust You to change my heart. Help me to act in love and trust. Instead of being annoyed or afraid or even really angry, please help me live like a girl who really trusts You. Please help my life reflect my love for You. In Jesus' name I pray, amen.

GOD IS MY HELP. HE STRENGTHENS
AND SUPPORTS ME.

ANGER ISSUES

Refrain from anger and turn from wrath;
do not fret—it leads only to evil.
PSALM 37:8 NIV

Father, I have an anger issue. Sometimes I get really, really angry and I don't deal with my feelings in a healthy way. I snap. I fly off the handle. I hurt other people with the things I say (or scream!) in the heat of the moment. I get so worked up and don't stop to calm myself down. It's almost like I feel good when I vent all of my anger in my words or through angry things I might do. Please help me turn from those angry responses. When I let myself rage, it doesn't help anyone. In fact, it actually can hurt me—and other people. Before I react in anger, please help me think through the consequences of my anger. Could I hurt someone? Could I hurt my own reputation? Am I overreacting? As I take that moment to consider what I'm doing, please help me find a way to settle down. I want to become more self-controlled. Please help me!

WHEN I'M ANGRY, I NEED TO CONTROL
MYSELF INSTEAD OF LASHING OUT
WITH ALL OF MY EMOTIONS.

BE ASTONISHED

"Look at the nations and watch—and be utterly amazed. For I am going to do something in your days that you would not believe, even if you were told."

HABAKKUK 1:5 NIV

Lord, You are at work every moment of every day. You are in the middle of doing something really big. So big, in fact, that I'd never believe it. Even though I can look around me—in my own life, in the lives of my family and friends, even in the world—I see Your hand at work. If I carefully pay attention to what's happening, I can be astonished as I see You working Your plan. I don't know how You orchestrate everything. And I wonder what You have in store. But one thing's for sure: You are doing something. And I wouldn't believe it even if You told me what You've planned. I worship You for being all-knowing and all-powerful! I love You!

GOD IS IN THE MIDDLE OF DOING SOMETHING RIGHT NOW THAT WILL ASTONISH ME. IN FACT, EVEN IF HE TOLD ME WHAT HE'S DOING, I WOULDN'T BELIEVE IT.

HOPE AND TRUST

For You are my hope, O Lord God.
You are my trust since I was young.

PSALM 71:5 NLV

Lord God, You are my hope! I trust You and confidently expect Your promises to come true. Hope means that I cherish a desire with anticipation—and I do cherish You and anticipate the way You'll show Yourself to be the Almighty God in my life. And You are my trust. I put all of my confidence in You—even my confidence for my eternity, which is pretty epic. Your Word has assured me that I can rely on You completely. I rely on Your character, Your ability, Your strength, and Your truth. I trust You! I'm so thankful that You've called me to be Your own even now that I'm young. I don't have to go through life wondering about You. I know You're real. I know You're living and working in my life. I know I can hope and trust in You. In Your name I pray, amen.

EVEN NOW WHEN I'M YOUNG,
I KNOW THE LORD IS MY HOPE.
I CAN AND DO TRUST IN HIM.

DEAD AND ALIVE

So you also must consider yourselves
dead to sin and alive to God in Christ Jesus.
ROMANS 6:11 ESV

Father, I want to be honest with You because You know all things. You know what I think and what I'll say, even before the words come out of my mouth. Because of that, nothing I confess or ask You is surprising. So when I tell You that it's really easy to sin, it comes as no surprise to You. And when I admit that a lot of times sin seems really tempting, that's also not a surprise. Lord, even though sin seems attractive, please help me consider myself dead to it. I don't want sin to have a grip on me. I want to get past my sins. I'd love to be alive in Christ. Dead to sin and alive to You—that sounds amazing to me. Please help me remember that I'm dead to sin when I face temptation. I love You and want to be alive in You! Amen.

I NEED TO REMEMBER I'M DEAD
TO SIN AND ALIVE IN CHRIST.

I WANT TO TALK ABOUT IT!

*My mouth will tell about how right and good
You are and about Your saving acts all day
long. For there are more than I can know.*
PSALM 71:15 NLV

O Lord, You are so good to me! Thank You! When I know You've answered one of my prayers, I want to share it with someone else. Please help me look for the ways You're good to me, and then tell about it. I want to say everything You do in my life. You've saved me from so much—from the punishment of my sins to the weight of feeling like I need to take care of myself or plan my own destiny—and I'm so thankful for that. Thank You for taking my burdens and heavy loads of trying to do everything on my own. Thank You for caring for me in a way so much better than I could ever do on my own. I pray that my thankfulness for You will bubble up every day in my speech. In Your name I pray, amen.

THE LORD IS SO GOOD TO ME. I WANT
TO TELL OTHERS ABOUT HIS GOODNESS!

MORE THAN I CAN UNDERSTAND

The peace of God is much greater than the human mind can understand. This peace will keep your hearts and minds through Christ Jesus.

PHILIPPIANS 4:7 NLV

Lord, Your peace is pretty amazing. It has an uncanny way of calming me down in even the most upsetting circumstances. I can trust You and relax. Your peace can and will guard my heart and mind. I don't understand how You do it. I just know You do. And I can't really explain what it feels like to rest in Your peace. But it's fantastic. I love when I don't have to worry or fear. When I trust You completely, You fill me with Your peace. Thank You for that wonderful gift! I know life would be a lot tougher if I trusted only in myself. And my life would be overwhelmed with worry if I didn't feel Your peace at all. Thank You for Your gift of peace that comes through Jesus! In His name I pray, amen.

GOD FILLS ME WITH HIS PEACE THAT'S BEYOND ANYTHING I CAN UNDERSTAND.

ALWAYS WATCHING OVER ME

*You have kept me safe from birth. It was You
Who watched over me from the day I was
born. My praise is always of You.*

PSALM 71:6 NLV

Father, You have a plan for my life. In fact, You've had a plan for my life since before I was born. That really blows my mind! Just like You've had a plan for me, You've also kept me safe. Thank You! You've watched over me every single day. Nothing has escaped Your notice. Even when I've had bad days, somehow they're part of Your plan, and You'll work all the bad details together for my good. I pray I'll listen to You carefully, and when I see You opening doors in my life or gently guiding me, I want to follow You and not rush ahead with my own intentions. I praise You for what You've done in me so far, and for what You still plan to do in my life. I'm thankful You're trustworthy. Thank You for watching over me and keeping me safe. Amen.

GOD HAS KEPT ME SAFE SINCE EVEN
BEFORE I WAS BORN. HE WATCHES OVER ME.

FORGIVENESS

*Because of the blood of Christ, we are bought
and made free from the punishment of sin.
And because of His blood, our sins are forgiven.
His loving-favor to us is so rich. He was so
willing to give all of this to us. He did this
with wisdom and understanding.*

EPHESIANS 1:7–8 NLV

Lord, I'm sorry I've sinned. I mean, I'm really, truly sorry. When I do things that seem particularly awful or unforgivable, I feel really guilty. And I feel so unworthy—especially unworthy of Your love. Even though those all are consequences of sin, You wanted to make a way to free me from the punishment of sinning. You sent Jesus to rescue me. Thank You! When I believe in Him, You forgive me of my sins and take away my guilt and shame. Through Jesus, I'm made free. Thank You! You are so loving and so kind to give me this freedom and forgiveness. Thank You!

THROUGH JESUS, I CAN BE FORGIVEN AND
FREED FROM THE PUNISHMENT OF MY SINS.

LOOK AWAY

Turn my eyes from looking at worthless things; and give me life in your ways.
PSALM 119:37 ESV

Father God, worthless things are all around me. But I don't always recognize them as being worthless. In fact, I usually think that they mean a lot. Sometimes I focus on my clothing or hair or shoes. And other times, it's tempting to think a lot about money or electronic devices or social media likes. I pray You'll turn my eyes from looking at those things. Please turn my mind from focusing on worthless things. Even if it means I'm different from others around me, I pray I'll start focusing on Your ways. Please help me think about things that really matter. I want to focus on what will last forever. And even if it will make me uncomfortable, please convict my conscience when I start focusing on things of this world. I love You and want to please You with my thoughts. In Your name I pray, amen.

GOD CAN HELP ME LOOK AWAY FROM
WORTHLESS THINGS OF THIS WORLD.

NO ANXIETY

Do not be anxious about anything, but in every situation, by prayer and petition, with thanksgiving, present your requests to God.
PHILIPPIANS 4:6 NIV

Father, anxiety has a funny way of creeping into my thoughts. Those anxious thoughts can ruin my attitude and fill me with fear and dread. I don't want those concerns and apprehensions to affect my life. I'm so glad Your Word tells me I shouldn't be anxious—in fact, I don't have to be anxious about anything! In every situation of every day, I'd love to pray to You about anything that's bothering me. When I'm tempted to worry, please help me bring those troubling thoughts to You. Thank You for listening to my requests. Because You care about me so much, my requests aren't silly or annoying at all. Thank You for loving me! Thank You for being the God who hears. In Jesus' name I pray, amen.

I DON'T HAVE TO BE ANXIOUS! WHEN I FEEL WORRIED, I SHOULD PRAY AND TELL ALL MY THOUGHTS TO THE LORD.

I WILL REMEMBER

I will remember the deeds of the Lord;
yes, I will remember your miracles of long
ago. I will consider all your works and
meditate on all your mighty deeds.
PSALM 77:11–12 NIV

Lord, You have done so much in my life. I don't ever want to forget how You've worked and the many ways You've blessed me. You show me favor time and time again. I'm thankful for the little things You do every day and the really big things that surprise me and bring me to my knees in thankfulness. By reading the Bible, I can learn about how You performed miracles in the past. But I can also think of the ways You've worked pretty miraculously in my life and in the lives of people I love. I want to remember Your mighty acts. I want to remember the way You provide in amazing ways. I want to remember all You've done. Thank You for choosing me, loving me, and working in my life. In Jesus' name I pray, amen.

GOD HAS DONE WONDERFULLY AMAZING
THINGS! I NEED TO REMEMBER HOW
HE'S WORKED IN MY LIFE.

WHO CAN UNDERSTAND MY HEART?

The heart is deceitful above all things and beyond cure. Who can understand it? "I the LORD search the heart and examine the mind, to reward each person according to their conduct, according to what their deeds deserve."

JEREMIAH 17:9–10 NIV

Lord God, You've created me and You know all things. Even what's deep in my heart and whatever's running through my mind. That could be scary, especially if I don't always like what I'm thinking or feeling. But in a lot of ways, it's also comforting. I may not be able to understand my heart—after all, it deceives and misleads me. And it's weak and frail. Jeremiah 17 even tells me that it's feeble, desperately wicked, and very sick. The thing is, so much advice from the world tells me to follow my heart. But I shouldn't! It would be foolish to trust something that's so weak and deceptive. I pray that I'll trust You instead. You want what's best for me, and I know I can trust that. As You search my heart and examine my mind, I pray You'll find that I'm devoted to You. I want to live a life that reflects my love for You. In Your name I pray, amen.

I CAN'T TRUST MY OWN HEART.
BUT I CAN TRUST GOD.

NO HOLDING BACK

*For the L*ORD *God is a sun and shield; The L*ORD *gives grace and glory; He withholds no good thing from those who walk with integrity.*
PSALM 84:11 NASB

Lord God, I'm astounded when I think of the way You give me grace and glory. You don't hold back any good thing from me if and when I walk uprightly. That means that when I'm living close to You, You fill my life with blessings. You protect me like a shield, and You shine over my life like the sun. I want to give over tomorrow—and every day!—to You with thoughts I think, words I say, and things I choose to do. Father, it's hard to live a sincere, innocent life. Especially when I see other people around me doing things that are pretty sinful, it's hard to not feel tempted to compromise. But I pray I'll stand strong. Please help me cling to You. When I do, You'll reward me in a way that's so much better than anything I could get from following what tempts me.

WHEN I LIVE IN A WAY THAT
HONORS GOD, HE WON'T HOLD
BACK ANY GOOD THING FROM ME.

BEING MADE RIGHT

*For Christ has put an end to the Law,
so everyone who has put his trust in
Christ is made right with God.*

ROMANS 10:4 NLV

Father, when I read the Old Testament, it's clear that You set so many laws for Your chosen people to obey. If I think of living by Your Law, I know I couldn't meet all Your requirements. In fact, I mess up every day! I'm pretty sure it's impossible for me to live one entire day without failing in some way. You knew Your Law was too impossible for humans to follow. And You wanted to make a way so we could be close to You. Even if we fell short from Your Law, You still wanted to make us right with You. That rightness comes through Jesus. I want to put my trust in Him! If I haven't before, I do right now. I trust that Christ will make me right with You. I trust that Christ has put an end to the Law so I don't have to worry about measuring up to a perfect standard. Thank You for Jesus!

WHEN I TRUST IN JESUS,
I'M MADE RIGHT WITH GOD.

THE DAY OF MY TROUBLE

I will call to You in the day of my trouble. For You will answer me.
PSALM 86:7 NLV

Father, some days are good, but other days are bad. Really, really bad. It seems like no matter what I do, from the time I wake up to the time I finally crawl into bed at night, one thing after another goes wrong. When I have those really, really bad days, please remind me that I can call to You! When I do, You'll answer me. You'll take my days of trouble and make them better. Thank You that I can pray to You at any time. I don't have to set up an appointment. I don't have to have all my words and thoughts planned out. I can literally tell You anything, wherever I am, whatever I'm going through. And on my bad days, I can vent to You and You'll listen and care. Thank You for being a bright spot and comfort to me on my darkest days! In Jesus' name I pray, amen.

WHEN I'M HAVING A REALLY BAD DAY, I CAN PRAY TO GOD. HE'LL LISTEN AND ANSWER!

PERFECT PEACE

You will keep in perfect peace those
whose minds are steadfast,
because they trust in you.
ISAIAH 26:3 NIV

Father God, perfect peace sounds amazing. In
fact, the thought of having perfect peace makes
me smile. Perfect peace means I'd feel complete
and whole. I'd feel safe, content, and calm. I'd
feel like my soul is resting. It's like I could take a
relaxing mental vacation from the worries and
stress of everyday life. The fantastic thing is that
perfect peace isn't impossible. And it isn't out of
my grasp. In fact, You will give me perfect peace.
When I trust in You and lean on You, You'll fill
me with Your perfect peace. My mind can rest
in You. I don't have to try to figure out ways to
be better or work for a more peaceful life. You
generously give it to me. Thank You! That's an
amazing gift!

WHEN I TRUST IN GOD,
HE'LL GIVE ME PERFECT PEACE.

RELIANCE

*Teach me your way, LORD, that I may rely on
your faithfulness; give me an undivided heart,
that I may fear your name.*

PSALM 86:11 NIV

Lord, thank You that You have a way that's unlike
any other way. Your way is true, and it's better
than any way I can try to create. It's better than
any way the world can offer. Because Your way
is the best way, I pray You'll teach me Your way.
Help me follow Your way instead of my own. As
I learn Your way, I pray I'll rely on Your faithfulness more and more. And I pray You'll change
my heart so it's completely united and joined
to You. Because You're so good to me, I want to
rely on You more and more. Instead of relying
on myself or on possessions or money, I pray
I'll rely on You for everything. It might seem
tough at first, and I know I'll be tempted to rely
on other things. But I really do want to rely on
You because You're so faithful. In Jesus' name
I pray, amen.

I CAN RELY ON GOD! HE'S FAITHFUL
AND CAN TEACH ME HIS WAY.

PLANS FOR ME

*O Lord, You are my God. I will praise You.
I will give thanks to Your name. For You
have been faithful to do great things,
plans that You made long ago.*

ISAIAH 25:1 NLV

Lord God, I praise You! You are the beginning and the end. You have created all things. You have a plan for all of time, and for whatever reason, You've planned for me to be part of Your story. You planned for me to be part of this world right now at this exact moment in history and in this exact place. You know every single one of my days, and You have good plans for my life. Even if some days Your plans might seem less than great, You've promised to redeem them and turn the bad things into good. Thank You! You are faithful to those You love, including me. I'm so grateful for that. I pray I'll be open to the way You move in my life as You work out Your plans. In Jesus' name I pray, amen.

THE LORD HAS A PLAN FOR ME!
HE IS FAITHFUL TO DO GREAT THINGS!

NUMBERING MY DAYS

Teach us to number our days,
that we may gain a heart of wisdom.
PSALM 90:12 NIV

Father, it's easy to feel like I have my whole life ahead of me. Days can go by so slowly, and weeks and months seem to go on and on. But to You, one day is like a thousand years, and a thousand years are like one day. Time flies for You! Instead of focusing on every little moment, You can see the whole big picture. You have a plan, and You're busily weaving all the details together, even if they don't make sense to me. Please help me remember Your timing for me is different from what I can fully understand. And please teach me to number my days and live like every single one matters. Even if it feels like I have all the time in the world right now, tomorrow is never guaranteed. My teenage years will fly by, so please help me make the most of them! Please help me use them for You. In Jesus' name I pray, amen.

I DON'T HAVE ALL THE TIME IN THE WORLD.
I NEED TO MAKE EACH DAY COUNT!

GENUINE LOVE

Let love be genuine. Abhor what is evil;
hold fast to what is good.
ROMANS 12:9 ESV

Lord, love is what should set Your believers apart from the world. Jesus taught that Your followers should be known by their love. Since I'm Your daughter, that command to love You and others is really important. I don't just want to fake my love and devotion though. And I don't want to turn it into a task I need to check off my to-do list. I want my love to be real and authentic. I want it to be genuine and sincere. When I have a hard time loving others, please work through me. I pray You'll fill me with Your Holy Spirit and let Your love flow out of me. I want to love and cling to the good in my day. If I see or hear or think of something evil, please help me flee. I want to live differently than most people out of obedience to You. In Jesus' name I pray, amen.

AS A FOLLOWER OF CHRIST, I NEED TO
BE KNOWN FOR MY LOVE! AND I NEED
TO HOLD ON TIGHT TO WHAT'S GOOD.

YOU ARE THE ONE

LORD, you are the God who saves me; day and night I cry out to you. May my prayer come before you; turn your ear to my cry.

PSALM 88:1–2 NIV

Lord, You are the God who saves me. Thank You! Thank You for Your concern for what's best for me. Thank You for paying attention to what's going on and for listening to my prayers. And thank You for stepping in and saving me! It doesn't matter when I pray—from early in the morning to late at night or even in the middle of the night—You are always listening. Even when my circumstances and situations are less than ideal, You're the One who hears and knows what I face. And You're the One who rescues me just at the right time. Thank You for the way You care for me. Please help me remember that I can always, always pray to You at any time, in any place, about absolutely everything. Nothing is too big for You to handle. In Your powerful name I pray, amen.

GOD IS THE ONE WHO HEARS
MY PRAYERS AND SAVES ME.

CREATED FOR A PURPOSE

For we are God's handiwork, created in
Christ Jesus to do good works, which God
prepared in advance for us to do.
EPHESIANS 2:10 NIV

Father God, any time I'm tempted to think poorly of myself—whether I failed a test or just lived through the world's most embarrassing moment—please remind me that You created me. You thought of exactly what You wanted me to be like. You knew what I'd look like, how I'd talk and laugh, what my favorite things would be, and what would drive me absolutely crazy. You planned it all because I'm Your creation. Your handiwork. You crafted me in this way. Whether I like myself or not, You made me just the way I am for a reason. And You created me to do good works that You've actually already prepared for me to do. Lord, please help me boldly do all that You bring my way! I don't want to feel too tired or scared or stressed. I want to step out in faith and do the good things You created for me to do. Amen.

GOD CREATED ME. AND HE CREATED
GOOD WORKS JUST FOR ME TO DO.

MANY THANKS

I will give thanks to You, Lord my God, with all my heart, And I will glorify Your name forever.
PSALM 86:12 NASB

O Lord my God, thank You! Thank You for creating such a beautiful world with changing seasons and so many unique plants and animals. Thank You for creating people with the ability and need to have relationships. Thank You for my friends. Thank You for my family members. Thank You for my church, my pastor, and all the people who serve so faithfully there. Thank You for teachers who take the time to help me learn, for giving me a place to live and food to eat and clothes to wear—for providing everything I need, and so many of my wants. Thank You for blessing me with unique gifts and abilities. And thank You for starting a relationship with me through Jesus. You are so very good to me and I want to praise and worship You with every part of my life. In Jesus' name I pray, amen.

THE LORD HAS BEEN SO VERY
GOOD TO ME! HE DESERVES ALL
THE THANKS I CAN GIVE HIM.

DAUGHTER OF THE KING

I urge you to live a life worthy of the calling
you have received. Be completely humble and
gentle; be patient, bearing with one another
in love. Make every effort to keep the unity
of the Spirit through the bond of peace.
EPHESIANS 4:1–3 NIV

Father, You have called me to be Your daughter. To thank You for that amazing gift—becoming a daughter of the King of kings!—I pray I'll be worthy of Your calling every day. May the words I say and the things I do reflect my relationship with You. Please help me be completely humble like Jesus was. Please help me be gentler in the way that I act and things that I say. Please help my patience grow, even when it's uncomfortable. And I pray I'll bear with other people. Even when they get on my nerves. Even when they don't treat me kindly. Even when I don't feel like it. With Your Holy Spirit's power, please fill my heart with Your peace so I can be united to other believers. Amen.

I AM A DAUGHTER OF THE KING OF KINGS.
I NEED TO THINK, SPEAK, AND ACT LIKE IT!

MORNING AND NIGHT

It is good to praise the Lord and make music to your name, O Most High, proclaiming your love in the morning and your faithfulness at night.

PSALM 92:1–2 NIV

Lord, thank You for Your faithfulness all throughout today. Thank You for faithfully blessing me in ways I didn't necessarily need or deserve. Thanks for making things better than they could have been. Even when I faced sticky situations, You had a plan, and You never left me. I praise You for always being there, ready to draw closer to me as soon as I start drawing close to You. Most High God, I'd love to experience Your love tomorrow morning. Please fill my heart with Your love and remind me of all the ways You've been faithful today. I don't want to take it for granted. And I want to look for You in every moment of my day, both big and small, really important and not-so-important. I praise You because You are my God! In Your name I pray, amen.

GOD IS SO GOOD TO ME! I CAN THINK ABOUT HIS LOVE IN THE MORNING AND HIS FAITHFULNESS AT NIGHT.

NOTHING I CAN DO

For by His loving-favor you have been saved from the punishment of sin through faith. It is not by anything you have done. It is a gift of God. It is not given to you because you worked for it. If you could work for it, you would be proud.
EPHESIANS 2:8–9 NLV

Lord, You give me so many good gifts that I don't deserve. But Your biggest gift is saving me from the punishment of my sin. Thank You that all I need is faith in Jesus. It's nothing I can do on my own. I could try to be a really, really good girl but never be good enough. And I could try to do good things every single day and never do enough. There's no way I can work to save myself. But through faith in You, I don't have to try to save myself. That's a very good thing! The way You love me and show me favor is pretty amazing. I don't feel like I deserve it, but I'll gladly accept Your gift! Thank You!

I CAN'T WORK TO SAVE MYSELF FROM
THE PUNISHMENT OF MY SIN.
BUT GOD CAN SAVE ME!

MY SAFE PLACE

I have a safe place in you, O Lord.
Let me never be ashamed.

PSALM 71:1 NLV

Lord, why are people so mean? I don't understand how people can say and do such mean
things. I feel ashamed when people laugh at
me. And when they say horrible things about
me or to my face, I feel awful. I hate knowing
that people say things behind my back. People
are hurtful. They're uncaring and unkind. They
don't think about how much they hurt my feelings. I pray I won't let their words or attitudes
affect the way I think about myself. You've made
me in a wonderful way. You've chosen me. You
never say bad things about me. You are my safe
place. I pray that when I'm tempted to listen to
what others say, I'll remember what You say in
Your Word. Thank You for taking all my sin and
shame away so that I stand blamelessly before
You. In Your name I pray, amen.

NO MATTER WHAT OTHERS SAY TO
ME OR WHAT THEY SAY ABOUT ME,
THE LORD IS MY SAFE PLACE.

THE OLD ME

*Put away the old person you used
to be. Have nothing to do with your old
sinful life. It was sinful because of being
fooled into following bad desires.*
EPHESIANS 4:22 NLV

Father, before I knew You, I was a different person. Even if I was a little girl, I lived a different life and had another destiny. My sin and unbelief separated me from You. I wasn't Your child. But once Jesus came into my life and saved me from the punishment of my sin, I became a new person. I became Your daughter. Your Holy Spirit came to live in me. I wasn't separated from You anymore, but united to You forever. I might look the same on the outside, but I'm a new person on the inside. Because You've made me new and changed me, please help me live to show those changes. I don't want to live like someone who doesn't know You. I want to make choices that reflect my love for You and live like I'm Yours. In Jesus' name I pray, amen.

BECAUSE OF JESUS, I'M NOT
THE SAME GIRL I USED TO BE!

WHERE'S MY FOCUS?

Seek the Lord and His strength;
Seek His face continually.
PSALM 105:4 NASB

O Lord, every day I'm faced with choices of what I'll seek. Do I want to seek my own pleasures? Seek what works out best for me? Seek what's comfortable? Seek what's popular? Or do I seek You? I have to admit it's a lot easier to focus on me instead of You. But I want to change. You've done so much for me that You deserve my life. Please help me readjust my thinking. Instead of focusing on myself, please help me start focusing on You. Even when it's uncomfortable or unpopular, I pray I'll seek Your will. What will make You happy? What will lift You up in front of the world? How would You have me love others? I know I can't do any of that on my own, Lord, so I pray You'll fill me with Your strength and help me know what would please You. I want to change my life so I'm seeking You! In Jesus' name I pray, amen.

INSTEAD OF FOCUSING ON MYSELF,
I NEED TO START FOCUSING ON THE LORD.

TELLING THE TRUTH

Rather, speaking the truth in love,
we are to grow up in every way into
him who is the head, into Christ.
EPHESIANS 4:15 ESV

Father God, it can be hard to speak the truth. I know honesty is what You want and expect of me, but it's hard! I don't want to be a liar. But sometimes, especially if people ask me to give my opinion, I don't like hurting their feelings. Or if a friend shares her deep, dark secret with me and I need to give a truthful response, I get worried she'll be offended or mad if I'm honest. In those times when it's really awkward but completely necessary to tell the truth, I pray I'll do it in a loving way. Please give me the words to speak. Help me to be loving and true, but not hurtful or offensive. Instead of insisting on using my own words to share my own thoughts and agenda, please help me to speak in love so I can become more like Jesus. In His name I pray, amen.

WHEN I SPEAK TO OTHERS, THE BEST WAY IS TO USE HONEST WORDS FILLED WITH LOVE.

HOW I WANT TO LIVE

Good will come to those who are generous
and lend freely, who conduct their affairs
with justice. Surely the righteous will never
be shaken; they will be remembered forever.
PSALM 112:5–6 NIV

Lord, so many days I rush through life and go through the motions. I do what I need to do at home and at school. I spend time with my friends and family. I don't always stop to think about the way You want me to live. But Your Word gives me plenty of direction! Your will for me is that I would be generous with others. I should be willing to give my time and attention and love and possessions. I can lend to people without expecting to get something back in return. And I need to live a just and right life. I shouldn't show favoritism to certain people, and I shouldn't try to get my own way. When I live like that, my life will be right in Your eyes. I'll be more like Jesus when I'm generous, loving, and fair. Even when it seems difficult, please help me live like that. Amen.

GOD ASKS ME TO LIVE A
GENEROUS AND JUST LIFE.

THIS IS THE WAY

Your ears will hear a word behind you, saying, "This is the way, walk in it," whenever you turn to the right or to the left.
ISAIAH 30:21 NASB

Father, I don't always know what I should say. And I don't always know what I should do. I want to do Your will, but I don't know what it is. When I need to make big decisions for my life, especially ones that will affect my future, I don't know what I should choose. Could You please help me? If Your Spirit directs me, please help me clearly know it's Him. I want to obey You. And I want to follow where You'll lead me. Please clear up any confusion, so I'm sure that You're definitely leading me to do a particular thing and that it's not just my own will. I want to obey and please You. But sometimes I'm not exactly sure how. Please clearly show me the way You've prepared for me and help me carefully listen to Your direction. I want to walk in Your way! In Jesus' name I pray, amen.

GOD WILL LEAD ME. I NEED
TO CAREFULLY LISTEN!

I LOVE YOU

*I love the LORD, because he has heard
my voice and my pleas for mercy.*
PSALM 116:1 ESV

Lord, I love You! I don't tell You often enough, but I do. I love that You love me so much that You wanted to bring me close to You through Jesus. Thank You for sending Him to this earth! And thank You that He was willing to be a sacrifice for me and my sins. I love You for hearing me too. You pay attention to my prayers. You're always there for me, always ready to listen. You hear my pleas for mercy, and You answer them. Thank You! Your timing and answers may be different than I expect, but You always do listen. And You always do answer. Just like You listen to me out of love, I pray that I'll listen to You out of love. I want to hear Your voice. In Your name I pray, amen.

I LOVE THE LORD! HE LISTENS
TO ME AND MY PRAYERS.

THE CALL TO LOVE

*The person who believes that Jesus is the
Christ is a child of God. The person who
loves the Father loves His children also.*
1 JOHN 5:1 NLV

Father, I do believe that Jesus is the Christ. I
believe He's Your Son and He came to this earth
to rescue people from the punishment of their
sins. And I believe that through Him, I can spend
forever with You. Thank You for sending Him!
I love Jesus. And I love You. As Your daughter,
You have a special job for me: I need to love
Your children in this world. It seems really easy
to love other believers I get along with. But for
others who get on my nerves? It's really hard to
love them. Even if and when I don't feel like it,
I pray I'll show them Your love anyway. Please
help me do it. I know I can't do it on my own.
I want to love unselfishly and sacrificially, just
like Jesus did. In His name I pray, amen.

SINCE I BELIEVE IN JESUS, I'M A
CHILD OF GOD. AS A CHILD OF GOD,
I'M CALLED TO LOVE OTHERS.

SUCCESS

Lord, save us! Lord, grant us success!
PSALM 118:25 NIV

Lord, I know You have the power to grant success to people. You can show Your favor and make things work out in a wonderful way. I pray You'll do just that in my life! Please grant me success in my school work. Please grant me success in my interests and activities. And please grant me success in my relationships. I pray I'll be a loving family member and friend. I'd love to bless other people so their lives are better because I'm in it. I pray for this success and favor not just for myself or my own comfort and pleasure. But I do want it to be obvious to the world that when I follow You and live in Your love, You not only save me, but You also help me succeed. If You have another plan for me, and if it doesn't seem like I'm succeeding right away, please help me learn patience and peace. But I don't want to give up. I want to persistently ask You. In Your name I pray, amen.

I CAN ASK THE LORD TO GRANT
ME FAVOR AND SUCCESS.

WORKING TOGETHER FOR GOOD

And we know that God causes all things to work together for good to those who love God, to those who are called according to His purpose.

ROMANS 8:28 NASB

Father God, I love You! And I'm so grateful You've called me to be Your daughter. You actually have a purpose for me and my life. And You chose me to be a part of Your plan. It's pretty amazing to realize that You make all things work together for my good. Even in the crummiest of times, when it feels like everything is going wrong, You'll find a way to make it right. Things may not instantly improve, but if I just wait, You'll surprise me with a happy ending. Please help me patiently wait for You and Your good things, Lord! Instead of feeling discouraged and down, please fill me with hope. I want to look for the good things You're doing in my life every day, no matter how big or small they may be. In Jesus' name I pray, amen.

GOD WILL MAKE EVERYTHING
WORK TOGETHER FOR GOOD!

TELL HIM ABOUT IT

Out of my distress I called on the LORD;
the LORD answered me and set me free.
PSALM 118:5 ESV

Lord, when I'm in trouble I can call on You. At any time on any day, You'll hear me. And when I'm having problems—whether I'm irritated or frustrated or facing serious difficulties—I need to tell You. You want to know what I'm thinking and feeling! I don't have to have answers, and I don't need my life to seem picture perfect. You know my heart, and You know the reality of what I'm facing. When I honestly tell You what I'm feeling, You can give me freedom! You'll answer me and put me in a really good place. When I keep my thoughts and feelings all bottled up inside of me, I'm missing out on the peace You long to give me. Thank You that I can come to You with complete honesty! In Your name I pray, amen.

WHEN I'M IN TROUBLE, I CAN—AND SHOULD!—
TELL THE LORD ABOUT IT.

REALLY GOOD THINGS

Yet the Lord longs to be gracious to you;
therefore he will rise up to show you
compassion. For the Lord is a God of
justice. Blessed are all who wait for him!
ISAIAH 30:18 NIV

Lord God, You are right and fair. You see me just as I am—You see past what I look like, what I wear, where I live, and what possessions I do or don't have. You look at my heart. You know what I think and how I treat others. Even as You know everything about me, You want to be kind to me and show me Your love. When I hope and put my trust in You, You'll fill my life with really good things that go way beyond anything I expect. You'll take care of me in amazing ways! I don't deserve Your kindness or Your favor. But I'm so thankful for them! Thank You for knowing me completely and loving me more than anyone else ever could. In Jesus' name I pray, amen.

GOD LOVES ME AND WILL FILL MY
LIFE WITH REALLY GOOD THINGS.

MY SAFE PLACE

Trust in Him at all times, O people.
Pour out your heart before Him.
God is a safe place for us.
PSALM 62:8 NLV

Father God, You are my safe place. Even if the worst things in this world happen and people start taking things away from me—my belongings, my freedoms, my safety—the one thing they can never take away from me is You. You will always be with me. And You will always be my safe place. Because You're always and forever my safe place, I can pour out my heart before You. When I get scared or sad, I can tell You every painful detail. When I'm angry and frustrated, I can fully vent to You. And when I'm thrilled and full of happiness, I can share every bit of excitement with You. I can trust You with every part of my life and know that You care about every single detail. No matter what, You will always be there for me. I love You, Lord!

BECAUSE GOD ALWAYS WILL BE A SAFE
PLACE FOR ME, I CAN TRUST HIM.

A NEW ME

*Let your minds and
hearts be made new.*
EPHESIANS 4:23 NLV

Father, sometimes I think about how fun it could be to get a makeover. What if I looked different? It might mean a new hairstyle or a change of clothing. But what if I could become a new version of me? If I looked like a new me, would I act like a new me? The amazing thing is that the thought of a makeover comes from You. You want me to become a new me! Even though I was born as myself, once I trusted Christ, I became a new person. Every day I have a chance to become a newer, better version of myself. You can make my mind and heart new. I don't have to feel stuck in my same old sinful habits. You can transform and change my life. I really do have a chance to live and act like a new me. Thank You for fresh starts! Thank You for new beginnings! In Your name I pray, amen.

THROUGH CHRIST, I CAN BECOME A NEW ME.
MY MIND AND MY HEART CAN BE MADE NEW.

I AM KNOWN

O Lord, You have looked through me and
have known me. You know when I sit down
and when I get up. You understand my
thoughts from far away. You look over
my path and my lying down. You know
all my ways very well. Even before I
speak a word, O Lord, You know it all.
PSALM 139:1–4 NLV

Lord, sometimes I wonder if I matter. Does anyone really know me? Does anyone even want to know me? You've already answered those questions in Your Word. And You are the One who knows me completely. You know everything about me. You know what I do and what I think. You know my habits and what I say. If I ever wonder if anyone can understand me, You can. In fact, You already do. If I ever wonder if anyone cares about me, You do. You know everything about me and love me completely. That kind of love and understanding is amazing! Thank You! In Jesus' name I pray, amen.

GOD KNOWS EVERYTHING ABOUT ME.
AND HE CHOOSES TO LOVE ME!

GOOD, NOT EVIL

Do not be overcome by evil,
but overcome evil with good.
ROMANS 12:21 NASB

Father, I know evil is a part of this world. In fact, I notice it around me every day. When I see what's going on in my community or listen to the news, I get discouraged and a little scared. I don't want evil and sin to have power over me. I don't want to do evil things, and I don't want it to fill my life with fear. I want to trust You and Your plans and purposes. And I want to be a light for You in the darkness. When I'm tempted to sin, please give me the strength to choose what's right instead. I want to do good—and keep doing good—in Your name. When I'm tempted to focus on what's going wrong, please refocus my attention on what's going right. Open my eyes to see all the good You're doing, both in me and in others around me. In Jesus' name I pray, amen.

I DON'T NEED TO FOCUS ON EVIL,
AND I DON'T NEED TO SIN. I CAN BREAK
THE POWER OF EVIL BY DOING GOOD!

WOW!

I will give thanks to You, because I am awesomely and wonderfully made; Wonderful are Your works, And my soul knows it very well.

PSALM 139:14 NASB

Thank You, Father! Thank You for making me just the way I am. And thank You for putting so much thought and care into who I am. You've made me in a wonderful way. It can be hard for me to believe that. I don't always feel wonderful. In fact, I can pick out all sorts of ways I'd love to be different. But I do know that You create wonderful things. I look all around me and can find beauty in the things You've made. Just like all of those beautiful creations, You've made me in a beautiful way too. Wow! Thank You! Please help me to start seeing myself as more of the wonderful person You've created me to be. In Jesus' name I pray, amen.

IT'S PRETTY AMAZING THAT GOD MADE ME IN A WONDERFUL WAY.

UNDERSTOOD

Because Jesus was tempted as we are and
suffered as we do, He understands us and
He is able to help us when we are tempted.
HEBREWS 2:18 NLV

Lord Jesus, it's really comforting to know that
You know how attractive temptation is. You were
tempted—maybe not in the same exact ways I'm
tempted, but You still understand temptation.
And You know what it's like to suffer too. Because
You were here on earth, You understand what I'm
feeling. You understand what I'm going through!
And You have the power to help me when I'm
tempted. Instead of minimizing that power or
forgetting that You're there to help me, I pray I'll
depend on You more. Please help me! When I'm
tempted, please remind me that I can stand up
under that temptation and avoid it. Just because
I'm tempted doesn't mean I absolutely need to
sin. I don't want to be a slave to sin! You've freed
me. Thank You!

JESUS UNDERSTANDS ME AND
THE ATTRACTION OF TEMPTATION.
HE CAN RELATE TO ME!

WHERE'S MY TRUST?

It is better to take refuge in the Lord than to trust in humans. It is better to take refuge in the Lord than to trust in princes.
PSALM 118:8–9 NIV

Lord, tonight I confess that I need to examine where I place my trust. Do I trust in myself and in my own gifts and abilities? Do I trust in my parents, my friends, or how my pastor, teachers, and school principals lead me? Do I follow community and government officials with a lot of trust? While all of those humans could possibly be good leaders, You are the One I should trust. You are the best option when I need to look for a safe place. You're my protection. You'll lead me the right way. You don't have to wonder what the best option is, and You don't have to make an educated guess, because You know all. Thank You for being trustworthy! I can trust You with my whole heart. In Jesus' name I pray, amen.

I SHOULDN'T TRUST IN HUMANS, BUT I CAN AND SHOULD TRUST IN THE LORD.

MY NEW SELF

Put on the new self, created after the likeness of God in true righteousness and holiness.
EPHESIANS 4:24 ESV

Lord God, thank You for the gift of Jesus! Thank You that through Him my old self is gone—my new self is here. The thing is, even though Jesus has made me new, I still have the tendency to slip back into my old, sinful ways. I want to put my old self away! You've created the new me to be right and holy like You. That seems pretty hard to wrap my brain around, but I'm still thankful for it! I pray that I'll put my new self on. Please help me to live a right life in Your eyes. And as hard as it seems that a girl could be holy, I pray I will live a holy life for You. Please help me be set apart for You, even in all of my normal, everyday life. In Jesus' name I pray, amen.

THROUGH JESUS,
GOD HAS MADE ME NEW.

I'M MELTING

My soul melts away for sorrow;
strengthen me according to your word!
PSALM 119:28 ESV

Father, I'm sad. And not just a little sad, but I'm feeling really upset. I'm so sad it feels like my soul is melting away inside of me. I feel blah and so down, and I don't know how to feel better. Please strengthen me! You are the lifter of my head—please lift my spirits too! I know there are good things in the world and many things I'm thankful for. Please help me focus on those. Help me see the amazing ways You take care of me and provide my needs. I choose to look for things You do that make me smile and remember all the good in my life instead of focusing on the negative. I believe my attitude and mood can change. Please help me make that change! In Jesus' name I ask all of this, amen.

WHEN I'M SO SAD THAT I FEEL LIKE MY
SOUL IS MELTING, I CAN TRUST THAT
GOD CAN STRENGTHEN ME!

HOLD ON!

*Let us hold on to the hope we say we have
and not be changed. We can trust God
that He will do what He promised.*
HEBREWS 10:23 NLV

Father, I definitely can act like I know what I'm talking about. I can say I have certain, churchy things in my life—I could say I have faith without really thinking about what that means. Or I could tell someone I'll pray for them, but not really mean it. I can also say I have hope in You without really acting like it. I want to start living out the things I say though. And even when I'm worried or scared or feel like giving up, I want to hold on to the hope I say I have. I want to hold on to my hope in You. I know I can trust You and You'll do what You've promised. But I want to start living like I really, truly believe that. Please let my hope and trust in You transform my life with Your peace. In Jesus' name I pray, amen.

I NEED TO START LIVING LIKE I REALLY
DO HOPE AND TRUST IN THE LORD.

YOU LISTEN WHEN I CALL

Because He has inclined His ear to me,
Therefore I will call upon Him as long as I live.
PSALM 116:2 NASB

Lord, when I call to You, You're ready and willing to listen to me. And You answer me. Thank You! I don't have to worry about remembering what I want to ask or tell You. And I don't have to come back at a different time when You're not busy. You're actually always ready to listen to me. Even when things are happening all over the world and countless other people are praying to You, You still know me and hear my prayers. That's absolutely amazing. YOU are absolutely amazing, and I praise You for Your power and greatness. Thank You for being the mighty God and still choosing to love me. I'm so humbled. In Jesus' name I pray, amen.

I WANT TO PRAY TO GOD THROUGHOUT
MY ENTIRE LIFE BECAUSE HE LISTENS
TO EVERY ONE OF MY PRAYERS!

FILLED UP

May the God of hope fill you with all
joy and peace as you trust in him,
so that you may overflow with hope
by the power of the Holy Spirit.
ROMANS 15:13 NIV

Lord, You are the God of hope. And when I trust in You and Your Son, Jesus Christ, the Holy Spirit lives inside of me and fills my life. Through Your Spirit, You give me all kinds of wonderful gifts like love, patience, and kindness. Your Spirit works in me to make me good, gentle, and faithful. You give me self-control and fill me with joy and peace. Those are such wonderful gifts! When I trust You and You fill me with Your joy and Your peace, my heart and my life overflow with Your hope. It's like I can't contain all Your goodness! Thank You! In Your name I pray, amen.

WHEN I TRUST IN THE LORD, HE FILLS
ME WITH HIS JOY, PEACE, AND HOPE.

KISSING FEAR GOODBYE

The Lord is with me; I will not be afraid.
What can mere mortals do to me?
PSALM 118:6 NIV

Lord God, it's such a comfort to know You're always with me. Always. Whether I'm awake or asleep, You're watching over me. I don't have to worry about what will happen. Even when it seems like things are spinning out of control, You are in control. Because of You, I don't have to fear. Please help me remember that when I'm facing a bully. When someone I consider my friend betrays me, help me remember You're always with me and for me. You know the truth. You know who I am. And You love me regardless of what other people say or do to me. Even if it's hard to not care about what other people think about me, please help me find my worth in You alone. In Your name I pray, amen.

I DON'T HAVE TO BE AFRAID
OF ANYTHING OR ANYONE
BECAUSE THE LORD IS WITH ME.

LIKE YOU LOVE ME

Be kind to one another, tenderhearted,
forgiving one another, as God
in Christ forgave you.
EPHESIANS 4:32 ESV

Father, thank You for forgiving me through Christ! Because I've been forgiven without deserving it, I pray I'll forgive others even if it feels hard. Because You've shown Your love and kindness to me, I pray I'll start treating others with love and kindness. And I pray You'll make my heart tender. Instead of becoming hard-hearted or calloused when I feel hurt or disappointed, please soften my heart. I want to treat others like You've treated me, with plenty of forgiveness and grace and love. Just like You look at me and see the real me who's deep in my soul, I pray I'll be able to look past the outside of people too. Please help me look past the things they say and do to discover who they really are. Then let me love them like You would. I need Your help to do this, Lord! In Jesus' name I pray, amen.

BECAUSE THE LORD LOVES ME AND
HAS FORGIVEN ME, I ALSO SHOULD
LOVE AND FORGIVE OTHER PEOPLE.

UNDERSTANDING

Your hands made me and fashioned me;
Give me understanding, so that I may
learn Your commandments.
PSALM 119:73 NASB

Father God, You've created me with a purpose—
I'm no accident. In fact, You made me in a completely unique way. Because You've made me
and You had a reason for my existence, I want
to communicate with You, Lord! Please help
me understand Your commands and Your will
for my life. I want to know what You've said in
Your Word, but I also want to understand it.
Sometimes it seems a little confusing to me. But I
pray You'll give me clarity and help me apply it to
my life. When I do, I know You'll fill my life with
good things. I'm thankful I can read the Bible—I
pray that I'll take the time to read it and let it
change my life. In Your holy name I pray, amen.

GOD MADE ME IN A UNIQUE WAY
AND HAS COMMUNICATED THROUGH
HIS WORD. I CAN ASK HIM TO HELP
ME UNDERSTAND WHAT HE'S SAID.

THE SAME!

*Jesus Christ is the same yesterday
and today and forever.*
HEBREWS 13:8 ESV

Lord Jesus, in a world where everything seems to constantly change, it's super reassuring to know that You never change. Never ever! You are the same today as You were yesterday. That's pretty amazing, considering You have always existed, even before anything else existed. You also are the same today as You'll ever be—forever. That's so comforting! I don't have to worry about knowing who You might be. You're constant. I can read about You in the Bible and learn all about what You said and did. I can learn about Your character and know that the same Jesus I'm reading about is my Lord and Savior. That same Jesus is You! I worship You and praise You for being the Son of God, and the Lamb of God who took away the sins of the world. In Your name I pray, amen.

JESUS CHRIST NEVER,
EVER CHANGES!

THE SWEETEST GIFT

How sweet is Your Word to my taste!
It is sweeter than honey to my mouth!
PSALM 119:103 NLV

Lord, Your Word is such a gift to me. It lights and directs the way I should go. It instructs me in what I should and shouldn't do. It teaches me about You and Your will. It tells me how You've miraculously worked throughout history. And, amazingly so, it's living and active so that it applies to my life and situations right now. It can cut to the heart of the matter and convict me of sin in my life. It's powerful and it comes directly from You. It's a sweet gift! Even sweeter than honey. Thank You for Your Word and the way it is absolute truth from You. I pray I'll read it more often, memorize it, and look for ways to apply it to my life. I love You and Your Word!

GOD'S WORD IS ABSOLUTELY TRUE
AND SUCH A SWEET GIFT TO ME.

RIGHT AND GOOD WORK

*The work of being right and good will
give peace. From the right and good
work will come quiet trust forever.*

ISAIAH 32:17 NLV

Father, sometimes it's hard to live right and be
good. But when I try to follow You and keep from
sinning, You'll give me peace. I won't feel guilty.
I won't regret things I've said or done. Instead,
I'll be filled with Your peace. And my trust in
You will grow into a really beautiful thing. Even
though I know I should choose what's right and
good, most times it's so hard! It's tempting to not
do what's right. And sometimes I'm not even
exactly sure if I'm making a good choice or a bad
one. Could You please help me? Please prick my
conscience when I'm tempted to do something
that's not right in Your eyes. I really want to
pay attention to You and obey—even when it's
difficult. Tomorrow, please help me wake up and
look for ways I can do good and be right. In Your
name I ask this, amen.

WHEN I DO GOOD AND CHOOSE TO BE RIGHT,
THE LORD WILL GIVE ME PEACE.

MY HIDING PLACE

You are my hiding place and my shield;
I hope in your word.
PSALM 119:114 ESV

Father God, sometimes when I'm scared or feeling so sad, I wish I could crawl away and hide. Sometimes I do by just curling up in my bed. Other times, I try to find a quiet place where I can be alone—it might be a closet, or a corner somewhere, or the bathroom, or even a lonely place outside. I can try to get away by myself when I'm feeling down or just need time away. In fact, Jesus did that a lot while He was here on earth. But when I do get away by myself, please remind me that You are my true hiding place. I can find a safe place of rest in You. You're my shield too—my protection. I want to put all my hope and trust in You. Thank You that I can run to You anytime and hide myself in You. In Your name I pray, amen.

WHEN I FEEL LIKE I NEED TO ESCAPE
THE THINGS OF THIS WORLD, I NEED TO
REMEMBER THE LORD IS MY HIDING PLACE!

DECISIONS!

If any of you lacks wisdom, you should ask God, who gives generously to all without finding fault, and it will be given to you.
JAMES 1:5 NIV

Lord, every day I'm faced with decisions. Some are small, but some are really, really big. In fact, some of my decisions will direct the rest of my life. I'm afraid if I make a wrong choice, I'll miss out on what You have planned for me. While some of my decisions obviously seem right or wrong, others seem to be okay. When my options all seem like they could be right, what I decide could change my life. What I should do once I graduate high school is a huge decision. Even the friends I keep or my choice to date or not to date can totally change my life for better or worse. Please help me make wise decisions! Please show me what's obviously wrong and help me wisely weigh all my options. I'm thankful that when I ask You for wisdom, You'll generously give it to me. Thank You!

WHEN I'M CONFUSED ABOUT THE DECISIONS I MAKE, I NEED TO ASK GOD FOR WISDOM.

WHERE DOES MY HELP COME FROM?

Where does my help come from?
My help comes from the Lord,
the Maker of heaven and earth.
PSALM 121:1–2 NIV

Lord God, You are the Maker of heaven and earth. You are the Creator of all—including me. Since You've made everything, You care about what happens. You pay attention to what's going on here on earth. You know what's happening to Your people. And You're willing to step in and help. You don't leave everything on its own. I don't have to fend for myself as I watch things spin out of control. No, You are here. I can go to school and get involved in activities and work really hard and have a ton of fun with my friends, and know You are right here with me. As You're with me, You're ready and willing to help me. Thank You! I'm so thankful I don't have to look for my own wisdom or strength as a way to help myself. I'm thankful that my help comes from You. In Your holy name I pray, amen.

MY HELP DOESN'T COME FROM MYSELF.
MY HELP COMES FROM THE LORD.

JUST DO IT

Do not merely listen to the word, and so deceive yourselves. Do what it says.

JAMES 1:22 NIV

Father, Your Word is true. And Your Word is filled with wise advice and commands. When I read the Bible, it's easy to see how I should live. You give plenty of clear instruction. The thing is, even when I know what You want me to do, I don't always obey. Making the choice to do what You command isn't always easy. In fact, sometimes it feels downright difficult. I want to do things my way, or I want to follow what someone else is doing. When that happens, I end up deceiving myself. I can know what Your Word says, but if I don't follow and actually do it, I'm only fooling myself. I need to do what You command, whether it's easy or hard. Even if I don't get to do something I really think I want to do, please help me obey You. Deep down, I really want to do what Your Word says. Amen.

IT'S NOT ENOUGH TO KNOW WHAT
THE BIBLE SAYS. I NEED TO DO
WHAT IT TELLS ME TO DO.

THANK YOU!

Give thanks to the God of heaven,
for His loving-kindness lasts forever.
PSALM 136:26 NLV

Lord God of heaven, I don't always take time to thank You. But tonight I want to stop and think about all the ways You've been so loving and kind to me. You created me for a purpose. Thank You! You called me to forever life through Jesus and have saved me from the punishment of my sins. Thank You! You've put me in a family and have blessed my life with friends. Thank You! You keep meeting all my needs in an amazing, generous way. Thank You! You've given me all sorts of unique gifts and talents. Thank You! You have wonderful plans for my future and will work out all things in my life for good. Thank You! I love You and I'm so thankful for Your good gifts! Amen.

GOD HAS GIVEN ME AMAZING GIFTS.
I NEED TO REMEMBER TO THANK HIM.

WALK IN LOVE

*And walk in love, as Christ loved us
and gave himself up for us, a fragrant
offering and sacrifice to God.*
EPHESIANS 5:2 ESV

Lord Jesus, thank You for loving me so much that You would give Your own life for me. I don't feel worthy of someone dying for me, but You had a different thought. You loved me so much You willingly made that sacrifice. Thank You! Because You lived Your life in love, I pray I'll follow Your example. I may not sacrifice my life for someone else, but I pray that I would be sacrificial in the way I choose to love other people. I pray I'll give up my own comfort and desires out of love for others. Please help me to walk in love and live every day of my life in love. I want to be like You! In Your name I pray, amen.

I WANT TO BE LIKE JESUS. BECAUSE OF THAT, I CAN LIVE A LIFE OF LOVE JUST LIKE HE DID.

NEVER LEFT ALONE

Where can I go from Your Spirit?
Where can I flee from Your presence?
PSALM 139:7 NASB

Lord God, thank You for the good gift of Your Holy Spirit. When I accepted Christ as my Lord and Savior, Your Holy Spirit moved into my heart. He lives there even now! Even if I didn't sense Him there today, I pray that You'll fill me with Your Spirit tomorrow and help me walk with Him. He's always, always with me, guarding me until I see You face-to-face. Because of that, I can't get away from Your presence, and that's a really good thing! You never leave me alone to face things on my own. I pray I'll be comforted by the way You're always there for me. And I pray I'll remember Your Spirit is with me! In Your name I pray, amen.

I'M NEVER ALONE. IF I'M A BELIEVER,
THE HOLY SPIRIT ALWAYS IS WITH ME!

QUICK AND SLOW

My dear brothers and sisters, take note
of this: Everyone should be quick to listen,
slow to speak and slow to become angry,
because human anger does not produce
the righteousness that God desires.
JAMES 1:19–20 NIV

Father, I admit I'm quick to do things the wrong
way. Sometimes I talk before I think about the
words I should say. Sometimes I act in the moment without thinking about consequences. And
sometimes I'm quick to think about myself and
forget about other people. Please change me
so I can become more like You. Please help me
become a better listener. Help me focus on others and hear what they say. As I'm working on
my listening, please help me change the way I
speak. Help me slow down and think about the
words I should say, and also how other people
might interpret the things I say. Also, please help
me control my temper. Instead of flying off the
handle easily, please help me calm down and
not be so offended or filled with rage. In Jesus'
name I pray, amen.

THE LORD CAN CHANGE ME SO I'M
QUICK TO LISTEN, SLOW TO SPEAK,
AND SLOW TO ANGER.

MY MASTER

See, the eyes of servants look to the hand
of their owner. The eyes of a woman
servant look to the hand of her owner.
So our eyes look to the Lord our God,
until He shows us loving-kindness.

PSALM 123:2 NLV

O Lord, I lift my eyes to You. I look to You, my loving and kind Master. You provide for me in ways I could never provide for myself. Yes, You give me material things like clothing and a home and food and other belongings. But You also give me things I could never buy—things like peace, joy, and hope that won't go away. I've looked for those things in this world, but apart from You I can't find them. The only thing this world has to offer passes by quickly. Thank You for Your good gifts that last. I pray I'll remember that You're my Master. I'm Your willing servant, bound to You by my love and thankfulness. I pray I'll look to You for direction and serve You willingly out of my love for You. Amen.

THE LORD IS MY MASTER. I LOOK TO HIM FOR
DIRECTION AND SERVE HIM OUT OF LOVE.

DARK TO LIGHT

At one time you lived in darkness. Now you are living in the light that comes from the Lord. Live as children who have the light of the Lord in them. This light gives us truth. It makes us right with God and makes us good.

EPHESIANS 5:8–9 NLV

Lord, before I knew You, I was living in darkness, apart from You. But once Jesus came into my life, You turned my darkness into light. I don't have to stumble and wander around this world like I'm in the dark. You've opened my eyes. I want to live in Your light. I pray the things I choose to do and say and think will reflect the fact that Your light is in me. Living in the light of Your love and following Your truth makes me good and right with You. I pray Your light will shine out of me into the darkness of the world. I need You to help me do that! In Jesus' name I pray, amen.

THE LORD HAS TAKEN ME OUT
OF THE DARKNESS AND BROUGHT
ME INTO HIS LIGHT. I NEED TO
LIVE LIKE I HAVE HIS LIGHT IN ME.

GOD'S PURPOSE FOR ME

The Lord will fulfill his purpose for me;
your steadfast love, O Lord, endures forever.
Do not forsake the work of your hands.
PSALM 138:8 ESV

Lord God, I love knowing You have a purpose for me and that You'll make sure You fulfill it. Sometimes I wonder what Your purpose for me is, but as I follow You step by step, You'll reveal Your will for me just at the right time. You do this out of Your steady, never-ending love for me. If I knew everything You had planned for me, I might feel overwhelmed or try to accomplish it all in my own strength. But when I trust You to reveal Your plan for me and work it out in my life, You will be the One at work. Please use me. And please don't turn away from me. I'm the work of Your hands, and I'm Your willing servant. Use me, please! In Jesus' name I pray, amen.

THE LORD HAS A PURPOSE AND A
PLAN FOR ME, AND HE WILL FULFILL IT!

DO NOT FEAR!

"For I am the LORD your God, who takes hold of your right hand, Who says to you, 'Do not fear, I will help you.' "
ISAIAH 41:13 NASB

O Lord my God, I love You! You hold me up in Your incomparable strength, and You hold my hand. You comfort me with Your love and care! You've told me not to fear. I believe You, and I know I can trust You. I pray that my trust in You and reliance on You will grow and grow. When I face trials, I want to lean into Your loving care without any fear. I can't wait to see the ways You'll help me. As I take courage in You and rely on Your strength, I can hardly wait to see what it will be like to live without fear. With You, I don't have to worry! With You, I don't have to fear! Thank You so much! In Jesus' name I praise You and pray, amen.

I DON'T HAVE TO FEAR.
THE LORD WILL HELP ME!

HEARING AND KNOWING

Let me hear in the morning of your steadfast love, for in you I trust. Make me know the way I should go, for to you I lift up my soul.
PSALM 143:8 ESV

Father, I'm so thankful for Your love! And I'm so thankful I can trust in You. Please comfort me with Your love tonight. Tomorrow when I wake up, please reassure me of Your love. Even if I wake up and need to hurry to get ready for my day, I pray You'll quiet my thoughts and my heart. Please remind me of how very much You love me—maybe it will be in someone's words to me, a song I hear on the radio, a beautiful sunrise, or Your still, small voice. I want to notice the ways You show Your love. I want to hear Your direction and the ways You speak to me. Please clearly let me know what way I should go. I want to please You with the things I say and do because I love You with all of my heart. Amen.

I TRUST AND FOLLOW THE LORD.
HE LOVES AND GUIDES ME.

COME CLOSER

Come close to God and He will come close to you. Wash your hands, you sinners. Clean up your hearts, you who want to follow the sinful ways of the world and God at the same time.

JAMES 4:8 NLV

God, sometimes I wonder where You are. When You feel far away from me, I wonder why. I forget that You seem far away because I'm the one who's far away from You. When I come close to You, You will come close to me. It's not like You chase me around, begging me to spend time with You. You quietly wait for me. I want to examine my life and get rid of sin that keeps me separated from You. I want it out of my life. When I get it out of my life by cleaning up my choices, I start following Your ways. I start drawing nearer to You. Please help me make the choices to stop sinning so I can have clean hands, a clean heart, and get close to You, Lord. Amen.

I'M THE ONE WHO NEEDS TO GET CLOSER
TO GOD. I CAN DO THAT BY GETTING
RID OF THE SIN IN MY LIFE.

GOING THROUGH A ROUGH PATCH?

For my eyes are toward You, GOD,
the Lord; in You I take refuge;
do not leave me defenseless.

PSALM 141:8 NASB

My Lord, I look to You for help! And I look to You for direction. I know You're my safe place, and I know You're my protection. When I'm in trouble, I want to come running to You for Your help and comfort. Even though I wish I didn't have to go through bad circumstances, I do know You're always there to guide me. Please help me learn more about You and about myself during rough times. When times are good, please help me remember how You've worked in my life and what You've taught me. I'd love for something good to come out of my trials, even if it's just the way You work in my heart. In Your name I pray, amen.

WHEN I'M GOING THROUGH A
HARD TIME, I CAN LOOK TO GOD
AS MY COMFORT AND SAFE PLACE.

ALWAYS GIVE THANKS!

Always give thanks for all things to God the Father in the name of our Lord Jesus Christ.
EPHESIANS 5:20 NLV

Father God, I thank You in the name of my Lord, Jesus Christ! Thank You for today and the way that You've worked in it. Thank You for the amazingly good things that happened. And thank You that I had the chance to trust You more and more when bad things happened. Thank You for the people in my life who cared for me and made my day better. Thank You for giving me some things I liked, whether it was my favorite food, or if I got something I've been asking for, or even if I got to watch or listen to something I like. Thank You for the little and big ways You've shown You love me all day long. I love You and I'm thankful for the way You show You love me! In Jesus' name I pray, amen.

I ALWAYS HAVE A
REASON TO THANK GOD.

HE KNOWS ME

Search me, O God, and know my heart!
Try me and know my thoughts!

PSALM 139:23 ESV

Lord God, You created me and You know me. Before a word is on my lips, You know what I'll say. Sometimes, I get a little scared at the way You know what I'm thinking. I'm embarrassed because I think things I don't want anyone else to know. But those secret thoughts of mine are no secret or surprise to You. You know what I'm going through, and You know exactly how I'm feeling and what I'm thinking. Instead of feeling ashamed or nervous about You knowing the real me, I pray that I'll willingly be an open book. Search me! Know who I really am. Know my thoughts. As You do, I pray You'll turn my heart to You. Please work in my heart in such a way that I reflect You more and more. Help me find comfort in You. As You prove Yourself faithful to me time and time again, I pray I'll trust You more. In Jesus' name I pray, amen.

**THE LORD KNOWS MY
HEART AND MY THOUGHTS.**

DON'T BE AFRAID!

*"Do not be afraid. For I have bought
you and made you free. I have called
you by name. You are Mine!"*
ISAIAH 43:1 NLV

Lord, when I look at the world around me, I could easily be filled with fear. If I pay attention to the news or try to figure out what's happening in current events, things seem scary and uncertain. So many people seem unlike me, and instead of celebrating our differences, it's easy to fear them. But You've called me not to fear. You've told me not to be afraid. Why? Because You bought me with Christ's innocent blood. Through His sacrifice, I was made free. I'm free from my sins and my shame, and I'm free from fear. I don't have to be afraid anymore. I am Yours. Yours! I'm a daughter of the King of kings. And You personally have called me by name. Out of all the people in all of eternity, You know me. Your loving care for me is so amazing. I'm so glad for the way You've set me free from fear. Thank You!

I AM THE LORD'S. I DON'T
HAVE TO BE AFRAID!

FILLED WITH JOY

The Lord has done great things for us,
and we are filled with joy.
PSALM 126:3 NIV

Lord, You've done really great things for me. Thank You! Your good gifts fill me with joy. You've forgiven my sins and given me freedom from my guilt and shame. You've saved me so I can spend my eternity with You. You've created me with a unique purpose and have a plan for my life. You've placed me right where You want me at this time and place in all of history. You've allowed my character to be sharpened by the people who surround me. You've blessed me with talents and abilities I can use for Your glory. Thank You! As I remember and appreciate Your good, loving gifts, I am filled with joy. In Your loving and generous name I pray, amen.

I'M FILLED WITH JOY WHEN I THINK
OF ALL THE REALLY, REALLY GOOD
THINGS GOD HAS DONE FOR ME!

HIS AMAZING GRACE

Grace to all who love our Lord Jesus
Christ with an undying love.
EPHESIANS 6:24 NIV

O Lord, the thought of grace is so beautiful to me. Grace. It's a gift of goodwill from You to me that fills my spirit with joy. Grace is Your mercy, love, and kindness lavished on me. Grace fills me with sweetness, pleasure, charming delight, and loveliness. Your grace turns me to Christ. It keeps and strengthens my faith in You. It fills me with knowledge of You and affection for You. Your grace is poured out and heaped upon me all because I love and trust Jesus Christ. You fill my life with so many wonderful things, and Your grace toward me is a perfect picture of the way You love me in a radically beautiful way. Thank You! I've done nothing to deserve Your love and favor and grace. But You've chosen to give it to me, anyway. Thank You! In Jesus' grace-giving name I pray, amen.

THE LORD FILLS MY LIFE WITH HIS
GRACE BECAUSE I LOVE JESUS.

THE LORD IS GREAT!

But may all who seek you rejoice and be glad in you; may those who long for your saving help always say, "The Lord is great!"
PSALM 70:4 NIV

Lord, You are great. When I think about all You've done and all You've promised to do, I'm blown away. You created the entire universe. You continually lead and guide Your chosen people all throughout history. You're so loving, kind, and great! When people seek You, You're found. You don't hide Yourself as an unknown god. You are the one true, living God. You are great! When I need Your help, all I need to do is ask You for it. You always listen, and You always generously give Your help. I don't have to worry about living on my own because You're always there for me. I don't have to worry about saving myself. You sent Your only Son, Jesus, to save me. Thank You! I worship and praise You. And I rejoice in You and Your greatness. In Your powerful name I pray, amen.

THE LORD IS GREAT! I KNOW THIS BECAUSE OF THE WAY HE'S WORKED THROUGHOUT HISTORY AND THE WAY HE'S WORKED IN MY LIFE.

MY DAILY DECISION

Come close to God and He will come close to you. Wash your hands, you sinners. Clean up your hearts, you who want to follow the sinful ways of the world and God at the same time.
JAMES 4:8 NLV

Father, every day I have a choice to make. Will I follow the sinful ways of the world? Or will I follow You? I can't follow both at the same time. I need to make a choice. And every day I do make a choice. I make choices with the way I spend my time and money. I make choices with my words and thoughts and actions. All of those clearly show what I choose: the world or You. Lord, You know the choices I've made today. I pray I'll look at tomorrow as a new start. When I wake up in the morning, help me begin again. I can follow You, or I can follow the world. Even if my choices seem difficult, they really all boil down to that. Please help me choose wisely. Amen.

I CAN CHOOSE TO FOLLOW THE WAYS
OF THE WORLD, OR I CAN CHOOSE
TO FOLLOW THE WAYS OF GOD.

FEAR FACTOR

*He will fulfill the desire of those
who fear Him; He will also hear
their cry for help and save them.*

PSALM 145:19 NASB

Father, when I think about fearing You, I get a little intimidated. To me, fear means being scared. And really, You're the God of the universe. When I think of Your power and might, I am a little scared! You are my loving Father, but You hold all of life in Your hands. Instead of only quaking in fear, though, I can also have a healthy respect of You. I know the power You have. I know You are the King of kings, the Lord of lords, the Mighty God. I worship You! As I recognize You for who You are—the living God of all and not a cosmic magician or genie in a bottle—I can praise You. You're my heavenly Father, and I'm Your daughter. As I worship You for Your greatness, You'll hear my cry, save me, and fulfill my desires. You're not just a powerful God. You're my loving, caring Father. I love You, Lord!

GOD IS SO MIGHTY AND POWERFUL. I LIVE
WITH A HEALTHY RESPECT AND FEAR OF HIM.

THE WAY I WALK

Look carefully then how you walk,
not as unwise but as wise, making the
best use of the time, because the days are evil.
EPHESIANS 5:15–16 ESV

Lord God, so many days I do whatever comes my way. I might have a daily routine, but I don't always have a daily plan. It's tricky to think about what I'd like to do and what I really should do. It's tough for me to think about how I can make the best use of my time. It feels like my entire life stretches out in front of me and I have all the time in the world. But my days are numbered. You know how many I have! I may not know how long I'll live, but I can walk through my days thoughtfully and intentionally. Please help me live wisely. I don't want to waste my time doing mindless things. Please help me use my time to do Your work in this world. In Jesus' name I pray, amen.

I CAN MAKE WISE CHOICES ABOUT WHAT
I DO IN MY LIFE AND HOW I USE MY TIME.

UNITED

I pray also for those who will believe in me through their message, that all of them may be one, Father, just as you are in me and I am in you. May they also be in us so that the world may believe that you have sent me.

JOHN 17:20–21 NIV

Father God, right before He was arrested, beaten, and crucified, Jesus prayed to You. He prayed for His disciples—and He prayed for me. In His last hours on earth, He prayed that future believers would be united. Unity was so important to Him because He was united with You. Just as You and Your Son were one, Your believers are supposed to be one, also. The unity of believers is so important so the rest of the world can believe in Christ. Father, there's so much disunity and fighting in the world today. I pray that Your believers would look past differences and focus on the only important thing that draws us together: Jesus. Please help me reach out in unity to other believers in Christ. In His name I pray, amen.

MY UNITY WITH OTHER BELIEVERS WILL POINT AN UNBELIEVING WORLD TOWARD JESUS.

OVERFLOWING!

May the God of hope fill you with
all joy and peace as you trust in him,
so that you may overflow with hope
by the power of the Holy Spirit.

ROMANS 15:13 NIV

God of hope, I trust You! I trust You with my life and I trust You with my eternity. As I trust You, You give me amazing gifts. You fill me with all joy and peace! You fill me with Your Holy Spirit. And with these beautiful gifts, I end up overflowing with Your hope. My heart and soul can't contain all Your goodness. Thank You for these gifts! They're so good and unlike anything I can get on my own. These good gifts of Yours fill and delight my soul. Thank You! I praise You for who You are and thank You for the hope You've brought to my life. As I sleep tonight, please fill my rest with Your joy, peace, and hope. I pray my life will overflow with Your goodness. In your precious name I pray, amen.

MY GOD IS THE GOD OF HOPE.
HE FILLS MY LIFE WITH JOY, PEACE,
AND HOPE UNTIL IT OVERFLOWS.

More Inspiration for Your Heart!

YOU MATTER

This delightful devotional, created just for teen girls like you, is a beautiful reminder of your purpose. . .your worth. . .your place in the world. 180 encouraging readings and inspiring prayers, rooted in biblical truth, will reassure your doubting heart. In each devotional reading, you will encounter the bountiful love and grace of your Creator, while coming to understand His plan—for you and you alone.

Flexible Casebound / 978-1-64352-520-4 / $12.99